T0317675

Japanese Equities

Japanese Equities

A Practical Guide to Investing in the Nikkei

MICHIRO NAITO

WILEY

This edition first published 2019
© 2019 John Wiley & Sons, Ltd

Registered office
John Wiley & Sons Ltd, The Atrium, Southern Gate, Chichester, West Sussex, PO19 8SQ,
United Kingdom

For details of our global editorial offices, for customer services and for information about
how to apply for permission to reuse the copyright material in this book please see our
website at www.wiley.com.

Wiley publishes in a variety of print and electronic formats and by print-on-demand. Some
material included with standard print versions of this book may not be included in
e-books or in print-on-demand. If this book refers to media such as a CD or DVD that is
not included in the version you purchased, you may download this material at http://
booksupport.wiley.com. For more information about Wiley products, visit www.wiley
.com.

Designations used by companies to distinguish their products are often claimed as
trademarks. All brand names and product names used in this book are trade names,
service marks, trademarks or registered trademarks of their respective owners. The
publisher is not associated with any product or vendor mentioned in this book.

Limit of Liability/Disclaimer of Warranty: While the publisher and author have used their
best efforts in preparing this book, they make no representations or warranties with
respect to the accuracy or completeness of the contents of this book and specifically
disclaim any implied warranties of merchantability or fitness for a particular purpose. It is
sold on the understanding that the publisher is not engaged in rendering professional
services and neither the publisher nor the author shall be liable for damages arising
herefrom. If professional advice or other expert assistance is required, the services of a
competent professional should be sought.

Library of Congress Cataloging-in-Publication Data is Available

ISBN 978-1-119-60366-5 (hardback) ISBN 978-1-119-60369-6 (ePub)
ISBN 978-1-119-60368-9 (ePDF) ISBN 978-1-119-60367-2 (Obook)

Cover Design: Wiley
Cover Image: © MarsYu/Getty Images

Set in 10/12pt ITCGaramondStd by SPi Global, Chennai, India

Printed in Great Britain by TJ International Ltd, Padstow, Cornwall, UK

10 9 8 7 6 5 4 3 2 1

Contents

About the Author

Michiro Naito began working in the securities industry in 1994, after graduating from the University of Texas at Austin with a Ph.D. in theoretical nuclear physics. His initial position was in the capacity of an equity derivatives strategist at BZW Securities Japan, where he primarily focused on convertibles and warrants markets. In the following years, he was hired as a Japanese convertibles analyst at Merrill Lynch in Tokyo, where he analyzed the convertibles market and instruments, and as an equities analyst at Teacher Retirement System of Texas in Austin, where he helped in making investment decisions with regard to Japanese, Korean, Taiwanese, and Australian equities. From 2004 to 2017, Dr. Naito worked as an equity derivatives/quantitative strategist at J.P. Morgan Securities Japan. His work involved analyzing the Japanese equities market as well as derivatives instruments. He also advised domestic and international investors, which included pension funds and hedge funds.

Acknowledgments

This book stems from my knowledge and experience as an equity derivatives/quantitative strategist and equity analyst specialized in the Japanese equities market. I was fortunate to work for some of the world's finest financial institutions—BZW Securities, Merrill Lynch, Teacher Retirement System of Texas, and J.P. Morgan—and my gratitude goes to them as well as to my ex-colleagues at those outstanding organizations for their friendship and support.

The success of the Japanese version of the book convinced me that there would be a worldwide demand for its English translation. In this regard, I am deeply indebted to Hiroshi Hanaoka of Kinzai for pushing forward with the Japanese version and to Tomoko Uetake of Thomson Reuters for serving as a bridge between Kinzai and me.

Last but not least, my utmost appreciation goes to Matt Holt, Gladys (Syd) Ganaden, Elisha Benjamin, Sharmila Srinivasan, and Amy Handy of John Wiley & Sons for believing in the value of this book and working on it to get it published in English. Because of their vision, this book can now reach investors around the world.

—Michiro Naito, Ph.D.

Preface

"Noise"

When we think of how the securities industry operates, perhaps the first word that comes to mind is "efficiency." The industry of elites, where bright minds and ample experiences go to war against one another in order to attain maximum profits and unimaginable wealth, may be the image conveyed by movies such as *Wall Street*.

In reality, however, transfer of knowledge and wisdom has not been executed very efficiently or smoothly in the securities industry. Some may point to a mountain of research papers written on a vast variety of subjects and say this is not so, while others may argue that modern technology has allowed us to amass a level of information unprecedented in quantity and quality. Indeed, bookshelves are filled with thousands of titles written on the subject of the securities market, stocks and bonds, and other financial instruments.

If we are to define knowledge or wisdom to be valuable and useful information, however, I am not at all sure how much knowledge and wisdom are actually being accumulated over time and generationally passed down in the securities industry. I worked in the securities industry for roughly a quarter of a century, and during my tenure, I heard the same questions asked and saw the same mistakes repeated over and over again. I believe that these facts alone constitute good enough evidence of "poor" transfer of knowledge and wisdom in the industry.

Richard Bernstein, the founder and CEO and CIO of Richard Bernstein Advisors and former Chief Investment Strategist at Merrill Lynch, in his book titled *Navigate the Noise: Investing in the New Age of Media and Hype,* said, "Investors are showered with so much irrelevant information, or noise, that the truly relevant information gets quickly buried or overlooked as being too obvious to be important. Investors probably need a great deal less information than is available to make an informed investment decision. More important, they need less information than they think they need" (Wiley, 2001, p. xii).

I cannot agree more with Bernstein. There are several reasons for the "poor" knowledge and wisdom transfer in the securities industry, in my view. First, the people who work in the industry are highly specialized and proprietary. In some sense, equity researchers, sales representatives, and traders are like professional baseball or football players. Although they share some traits, their skills and know-how are often unique and cannot be easily shared. In addition, since their accumulated knowledge is their proverbial bread and butter, they have little incentive to readily dispense it.

The second reason somewhat overlaps the first, but the very nature of the securities industry hinders the generational bridging of knowledge and wisdom. By this, I am alluding to the rather quick and abrupt turnover of employees. The securities industry is well known not only for its oversized paychecks but also for its propensity to restructure at will, as the market goes up and down. Employees are typically given little notice before receiving pink slips, and thus there is no time to pass down what they know to the next generation of employees (and even if they have the time, they may not do so for the reasons stated in the previous paragraph).

The third reason is twofold: information overload and the size of the paycheck itself. On a daily basis, as Mr. Bernstein puts it, "Investors are showered with so much irrelevant information, or noise." On the other hand, brokers are getting paid handsome salaries by simply disseminating the "noise." Why would brokers bother to judge what is important and what is not if they are getting paid by distributing noise? Needless to say, the responsibility also lies with investors. This is because if investors like noise, brokers are almost obliged to supply them with noise.

Fourth, on the surface, the ever-changing nature of the market makes it difficult to discern what is relevant or important. The market is a mirror of the economy and collective sentiment of the people who participate in it. As such, the market is a "living" thing and thus evolves constantly. On the surface, therefore, there is no universal or natural law that governs the market into eternity. I have intentionally emphasized the phrase "on the surface" here. Although there is probably no "eternal" law, there are myriad laws and patterns that govern the market at least for some extended period of time, in my view. It may be difficult to uncover these laws and patterns, but with some effort, it can be done.

The motivation for writing this book is to transfer what I learned about the Japanese equity market through years in the industry. I worked for BZW Tokyo from 1994 to 1997, Merrill Lynch Japan from 1998 to 2000, Teachers Retirement System of Texas from 2000 to 2003, and J.P. Morgan Japan from 2004 to 2017. Having worked in the capacity of equity derivatives strategist during most of these periods, I saw the market from both the top down and the bottom up.

I lived through the aftermath of the collapse of the 1980s colossal Japanese bubble and saw the spectacular rise of the Japanese equity market during the internet bubble. I experienced the 2005–2007 global credit bubble, the subsequent market crash of 2008–2009, and the effect on the stock market of the Fukushima nuclear accident induced by the Great East Japan Earthquake in 2011. The next big thing for Japan was "Abenomics," which effectively began at the end of 2012, and I am now privileged to witness what the Japanese equity market will do in light of Brexit in the UK and Donald Trump's presidency in the US.

What is written here stems from the accumulation of facts and ideas from all those periods. In this regard, this is a history book as well as a guidebook, although the focus is on the period since 2004, after I began working for J.P. Morgan Japan. Also, this book is not a typical "Equity 101" book. I will not tell you how to pick "good stocks" in general terms. In fact, I am not even sure if picking "good stocks" works all that well in Japan (Warren Buffett may disagree on this point).

While some of the subjects covered in the book may be of historical interest and value only, these were significant at the time and were surely not "noise." To understand these historical facts and the lessons learned from them should no doubt benefit future generations of investors. What I have tried to do is lay out a simple map of investing in Japanese equities, with a belief that the paths depicted on this map may indeed help attentive and shrewd investors pave their own paths to enormous wealth.

On business trips overseas, some investors told me that they would not invest in Japanese equities because of the nation's shrinking population and lack of structural reform. While over a very long period of time their views may prove wise, that is not how you make money in equities. In my view, the Japanese equity market, when timed correctly, offers the best money-making opportunities among any major developed markets. I hope, by reading this book, investors will be able to take advantage of these fantastic opportunities in the future.

History Repeats Itself

"The Japanese equity market, when timed correctly, offers the best money-making opportunities among any major markets" is the assertion made in the last section. Whether we trade equities or other assets, the basic rule is to "buy low and sell high." In this sense, the above assertion is not an earth-shaking statement. The issue is to know the proper "timing" of the trade.

The reason the Japanese equity market "offers the best money-making opportunities" is that proper "timing" is relatively easy to identify. This is because the Japanese equity market, among major developed markets in the world, responds most sensitively to the global economic conditions, a tendency largely unbroken since the early 1990s.

Analysts knowing the stock market is similar to doctors knowing illnesses. The stock market is ever-changing, but what is underneath are human thoughts and behaviors, just as human blood and genes play a major role in identifying illnesses. And just as doctors refer to past cases to find remedies, we need to reflect on past incidents to respond to the elusive stock market.

This is the reason why I consider this book "a history book," because it is a book of case studies. The various indicators and indices that we may learn about in a textbook only come alive in the context of history. Whether macro indicators or seasonality, the reason we focus on them is because they have been useful over significant time. Otherwise, they are just "noise."

As long as the equity market follows the trail of corporate profits, it is a reflection of the economy. If we know which way the economy is headed, therefore, we should know which way the equity market is headed. And knowing historical patterns helps us predict the direction of the economy to a large extent.

The short-term fluctuations of the equity market are not necessarily due to the economy, however. What is needed in forecasting short-term moves is an understanding of the "time" or "current," as those are often caused by "events." The word "events" refers not only to policy decisions and natural disasters, but also to supply-demand imbalance, leading to sudden fluctuations in the market. Once again, turning the pages of history should help us properly grasp the influence of these "events."

Needless to say, history does not enable us to know the direction of the equity market 100%. "History repeats itself" is only a figure of speech, since after all, time flows only in one direction and the past is never exactly the same as the present or the future. But the importance of knowing history cannot be emphasized enough. If buy-low/sell-high is the basic principle of equity investing, then knowing the proper timing is all there is to it, and knowing history generally leads to more accurate assessment of the timing.

Clearly, I do not claim to know all the causes and effects of the past events. What is written here are the conclusions I've reached from my experience and analysis and, to that extent, probably does not represent the full picture. This said, the picture drawn here is perhaps more insightful than most and should aid in guiding investors through a complex territory called the Japanese equity market.

CHAPTER 1

Macro Indicators and Seasonality

I f the equity market is a reflection of the economy, then what can tell us about the state of the economy? The answer lies in macro indicators. Here, we focus on those I believe to be the most effective when used with the Japanese equity market, the OECD CLI and Economy Watchers' DI, and those perhaps less effective but nevertheless important, ISMPMI and seasonality.

OECD CLI

OECD CLI stands for *Organization of Economic Co-operation and Development Composite Leading Indicators*, which are the series of macroeconomic indicators released monthly by the OECD. Since an in-depth explanation of how these indicators are constructed and calculated is beyond the scope of this book, interested readers should refer to the relevant section on the OECD homepage (http://www.oecd.org/sdd/leading-indicators/).

The OECD CLIs were originally developed by the OECD to forecast the peaks and valleys of the economy. The history of CLIs goes back to the 1960s, and throughout the years since, the OECD has endeavored to examine and improve the accuracy of these indicators. At present, CLIs are published for each of the OECD member countries, as well as for larger economic regions.

More concretely, the CLIs result from the collection of economic data released by the member nations, and thus, the figures calculated monthly are released about a month and ten days after the fact (e.g., a January number is usually released around March 10). We may wonder how effective *leading indicators* can be if the release of the number is delayed that much. The fact of the matter is that even though the numbers are released about a month and ten days late, the OECD CLIs still function as the leading indicators.

Because there are many CLIs corresponding to each OECD member nation and various regions, the question is which one of them is the most effective in forecasting the direction of the Japanese equity market. To my knowledge, the answer is the G7 OECD CLI, which was developed to predict the direction of the G7 economy. Table 1.1 lists the weight allocated to the G7 countries in the CLI and which time series are used for each country to calculate the monthly CLI.

TABLE 1.1 G7 OECD CLI component countries and weights, and time series used

Country	Country Weight	Indices
USA	49.95%	Dwelling started
		Durable goods new orders
		Share price index
		Consumer sentiment
		Weekly hours of work
		Purchasing managers index
		Interest rate spread
Japan	13.98%	Inventories to shipment ratio
		Import/Export ratio
		Loans/Deposits ratio
		Monthly overtime hours
		Dwelling started
		Share price index
		Interest rate spread
		Small business survey
Germany	10.74%	Business climate
		Orders inflow/demand
		Export order
		Total new orders
		Finished goods stocks
		Interest rate spread
UK	7.51%	Business climate
		New car registration
		Consumer confidence
		3-month eligible bank bills
		Production future tendency
		Finished goods stocks
		FTSE nonfinancial share price
France	7.30%	New car registration
		New job vacancies
		Consumer confidence

TABLE 1.1 (*Continued*)

Country	Country Weight	Indices
		Eonia interest rate
		Interest rate spread
		Production future tendency
		Industrial sector prospects
		Finished goods stocks
		SBF 250 share price index
		Terms of trade
Italy	5.95%	Consumer confidence
		3-month interbank rate
		Production future tendency
		Deflated net new orders
		Order books or demand
		Terms of trade
Canada	4.56%	Deflated money supply
		Housing starts large cities
		US purchasing managers index
		Consumer confidence
		Interest rate spread
		Inventories to shipment ratio
		Share price index

Source: OECD

The OECD homepage has a further and detailed description of this CLI, and the monthly time series since January 1959 can be downloaded here: https://stats.oecd.org/Index.aspx?queryid=6617#

A major word of caution is needed when using the time series, however: Investors need to use the deviation from the 1-year moving average of the original time series. When the deviation is in a positive direction from the moving average, the market is a "buy," and otherwise the market is a "sell." This simple process is an amazingly effective formula in trading the Japanese equity market.

In the 25-year period of September 1991 to August 2016, by hypothetically trading TOPIX futures according to the above prescription, the

TABLE 1.2 Trading TOPIX by G7 OECD CLI

Cumulative Return	Average Return	Stdev	Win Ratio
2083.20%	11.70%	19.70%	72.00%

Sources: OECD, TSE

"win ratio" (the percentage of positive returns from the buy-sell process) is over 72% and the cumulative return is about 2100% (Table 1.2). Roughly speaking, had we invested JPY10 million in TOPIX futures at the beginning of 1990, the investment would have generated JPY210 million by August 2016. Had we just held on to TOPIX futures during the same period, the return could have been negative (depending on the exact dates). Because the Nikkei 225 (or the "Nikkei") moves largely in unison with the TOPIX, similar results should be attained by trading Nikkei futures by the OECD CLI.

I do not expect readers to accept this claim on face value. Those skeptical are advised to download the aforementioned G7 OECD CLI time series onto Excel and conduct their own backtest. What needs to be done is to calculate the return, assuming that TOPIX was traded based upon the "buy" and "sell" signals attained from the indicator.

Here, a few salient points should be mentioned. The OECD homepage lists multiple G7 OECD CLI time series. Each is calculated using different methods, but the time series to be used for the backtest are those of *the Amplitude-adjusted CLI*. For generation of appropriate signals, a 1-year moving average of this time series data should be employed.

Additionally, the results obtained by performing this backtest may not be the exact replica of Table 1.2. The reason, as explained below, is that the OECD habitually revises the time series, and thus the current time series may differ from the time series used to calculate Table 1.2. Consequently, the peaks and troughs of the economy may shift by a month or so, but that does not affect the long-term performance of the CLI (Figure 1.1).

We also need to take note that this indicator does not function well pre-1990. The Japanese equity market during the 1980s was the "bubble" market, which, by definition, tends to defy economic conditions. And the Japanese economy before the '80s, except for the hyperinflationary periods due to the "oil shocks," is largely characterized by high growth, and thus was generally not in tune with global economic conditions.

FIGURE 1.1　Peaks and troughs calculated from G7 OECD CLI and TOPIX

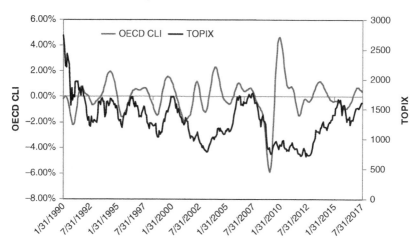

Sources: OECD, TSE

As for the revision of the time series, as mentioned above, the CLI is calculated from a collection of economic data provided by each nation. Accordingly, often the original economic data may not become available in time for its first release or be revised by the source after first release (governments often revise their economic data). In addition, since the OECD employs a normalization algorithm in calculating the CLI, the past time series may not match the present ones.

If the time series data is revised on a monthly basis, its validity in capturing the economic reality of the time may seem questionable. The OECD, however, in response to this concern, conducted an extensive examination a few years ago and came to the conclusion that frequent revisions of the time series do not engender significant errors in the judgment of economic peaks and troughs. What this means is that the effectiveness of the CLI examined as of ten years ago, for example, does not vary greatly from the effectiveness of the CLI ten years ago examined by using the current time series data.

Table 1.3 is the result of hypothetically trading TOPIX futures by using the G7 OECD CLI signals generated by the time series frozen at one arbitrary point in time. In addition, from 2004 on, the "real-time" data points, as they were released by the OECD, were used for the return calculation (in other words, the results are not affected by the time series alteration).

In the table, "Period" refers to the span of time where the OECD CLI signal was either going up or coming down, "Long Return" denotes the return by holding the TOPIX long, and "Short Return" denotes the return by shorting the TOPIX. In reality, returns were calculated assuming that TOPIX long and short positions are alternately held.

As the "Win Ratio" of over 70% suggests, we see more positive returns than negatives. Also, whenever there were significant market moves, the OECD CLI signals were able to capture them. This is particularly notable during the internet bubble of the late 1990s, the Koizumi bull market of mid-2005 to mid-2006, the 2007–2008 Global Financial Crisis, and the Abenomics bull market from late 2012 onward.

Since the OECD CLI is an economic indicator, when unexpected events not attributable to the economy take place, the signals generally suffer inferior returns. Most of the negative returns recorded in Table 1.3 are of this category.

For example, the return well below 10% from May 1997 to October 1997 (TOPIX futures bought following the OECD CLI "buy" signal ended in a loss) is a direct result of the outbreak of the Asian Financial Crisis in July of that year. We also see over 20% loss by holding TOPIX long from June 2001 to July 2002. The loss is due to the collapse of the internet bubble and 9/11.

The cases where losses were incurred by holding the TOPIX short tend to be related to policy actions. A good example of this is the −14% return recorded from February 2014 to January of the next year. In this case, in order to stimulate the ailing economy of the time, the Bank of Japan (BoJ) launched the second campaign of quantitative easing (QE) on October 31, and on the same day, the Government Pension Investment Fund (GPIF) announced its major asset allocation change, boosting equity weight to an unprecedented level. In other words, the market rose on the hopes and expectations based on the potential consequences of these policy changes, ignoring the weak economic reality.

While this manuscript was being written, at the end of October 2017, despite the OECD CLI signal that had turned negative in May of the same year, the Japanese equity market continued to rise. We could identify several reasons for this.

First, the US equity market was robust, which apparently stemmed from the signs of the recovery of US economic health and hopes for

TABLE 1.3 Trading TOPIX futures by OECD CLI

Period	Long Return (%)	Short Return (%)
12/10/91–1/11/93		23.84
1/11/93–8/10/94	29.43	
8/10/94–9/11/95		12.45
9/11/95–12/10/96	5.84	
12/10/96–5/12/97		3.02
5/12/97–10/13/97	−10.58	
10/13/97–11/10/98		19.50
11/10/98–12/10/99	50.35	
12/10/99–6/11/01		19.37
6/11/01–7/10/02	−20.24	
7/10/02–5/12/03		19.06
5/12/03–2/10/04	23.06	
2/10/04–7/11/05		−15.49
7/11/05–5/12/06	41.91	
5/12/06–12/11/06		2.51
12/11/06–7/10/07	9.44	
7/10/07–4/10/09		51.40
4/10/09–3/5/10	7.88	
3/5/10–1/11/11		−0.38
1/11/11–4/11/11	−8.60	
4/11/11–1/12/12		13.37
1/12/12–7/9/12	4.39	
7/9/12–11/9/12		4.63
11/9/12–10/9/13	60.58	
10/9/13–1/14/14		−8.50
1/14/14–2/10/14	−6.29	
2/10/14–1/13/15		−14.03
1/13/15–4/9/15	16.75	
4/9/15–1/12/16		12.22
1/12/16–2/8/16	−2.94	
2/8/16–4/11/16		7.29
4/11/16–5/10/17	23.86	

Sources: OECD, TSE

massive tax cuts. Second, the Chinese economy, not part of the G7 OECD CLI, was strong. Third, there was a landslide victory for the ruling Liberal Democratic Party (LDP) in Japan's lower house election held on October 22. Fourth, there were significant monetary policy differences between the US and Japan (to be discussed in later chapters).

Indeed, the total OECD CLI, which includes China, turned up in August 2017 and was able to capture the upside between then and October. Whether we are witnessing a paradigm shift of some sort, where the G7 OECD CLI may no longer be effective in the world of super-low interest rates and increasing Chinese influence, remains to be seen.

More on OECD CLI

To understand and appreciate the validity of the OECD CLI, perhaps a further elaboration is justified. As stated earlier, the G7 OECD CLI is a collection of economic data from each of the G7 member nations. For its calculation, the data sets are weighted roughly in proportion to the GDP of the member nations (the weights are reviewed occasionally).

The US, with the largest GDP, has about 50% weight in the indicator and therefore is the most influential. The US equity market (more specifically, the S&P500) has low sensitivity to the G7 OECD CLI, however. Not only that, but even the sensitivity to the American OECD CLI is low. In other words, the OECD CLI is effective with the Japanese equity market but not with the US equity market.

To repeat, the Japanese equity market before 1990 also had low sensitivity to the OECD CLI. Viewed long-term, equity markets tend to follow nominal GDP growths, and thus, if the GDP is growing constantly, the equity market should grow constantly as well. Accordingly, the difference in the US-Japan GDP growth rates are reflected in the equity market performance of the two nations.

In the last quarter century, the US equity market saw large downturns only twice, precipitated by the collapse of the internet bubble and the 2007–2008 Global Financial Crisis (GDP suffered simultaneously). The rest of the time, the US equity market has largely sloped upward, showing insensitivity to the OECD CLIs, which are designed to capture the "change" in the economy. Put simply, the US, with its almost constantly growing GDP, and Japan, with its fluctuating GDP, understandably exhibit differing patterns in their respective equity market behaviors.

"Buy and hold" refers to an investment strategy where investors buy the asset at one point in time and hold it for some period. This strategy is generally effective in the US equity market. Had we held on to the S&P 500 Index (by renewing futures contracts) since the early 1990s, the return would have been over 700%, but had we done the same with TOPIX futures, as mentioned earlier, the return would have been mediocre at best. No wonder US equity investors generally have "faith" in their equity market.

Incidentally, regarding the GPIF's major asset allocation change at the end of October 2014, briefly touched upon earlier, the investment community was surprised by this bold move, since the 12% weight previously allocated to domestic equities was elevated to 25% (50% equity weight including foreign equities). This "event" will be a subject of discussion later in this book, but the GPIF's move was undoubtedly patterned after US pension funds, which generally allocated well over 50% of their assets to equities.

Funds exposed to the upward-sloping US equity market and funds exposed to the up-and-down high volatility Japanese equity market perhaps deserve different asset allocations and treatments, because any long-term returns of the two markets would be divergent. Whether the GPIF management paid enough attention to the varying characteristics of the two markets is questionable, however.

Going back to the main theme of this section, since Japan is a member nation of the OECD, the organization also calculates the Japanese OECD CLI. Since the Japanese OECD CLI is uniquely geared toward Japan, we might expect the Japanese equity market to be more sensitive to this CLI than to the G7 OECD CLI. The reality, however, is that the Japanese equity market has behaved more in tune with the G7 OECD CLI (using the deviation from the 1-year moving average of the original time series).

Anyone who has studied the Japanese equity market should know that foreign investors play a major role in determining the market's direction (to be discussed in detail later in this book). Since the 1990s, roughly two-thirds of the daily trading volume has been attributed to foreign investors, and this number alone is a testament to their dominance. It is a little-known fact, however, that the weekly foreign investors' net transaction data released by the Tokyo Stock Exchange (TSE) largely coincides with the divergence from the 1-year moving average of the G7 OECD CLI, the very indicator under consideration.

This is not to say that every foreign investor follows the OECD CLI when trading Japanese equities. Rather, it is reasonable to assume that macro funds and others that trade equity futures probably time their investments by some sort of macroeconomic indicators (one of which could be the OECD CLI). In fact, the grapevine says that a world-famous hedge fund once used the G7 OECD CLI in trading Japanese equities during the '90s and never saw a year with a negative return.

Since the OECD CLI is an economic indicator, we would not be surprised to see its effectiveness with other assets outside of equities, as long as the asset price follows the economy. In this category, I have only tested the oil price against the G7 OECD CLI, but other commodity prices are likely to follow a more or less similar path.

As for the oil price, the backtest was conducted very much the same way as the backtest done with the TOPIX. From the beginning of 2001 to the end of 2013, the win ratio was an impressive 76% and the cumulative return was 1045%. The result may not be too surprising, however, as it only says that the oil price is sensitive to global economic conditions.

"If the OECD CLI is so important, can't we know the number before its release?" is a fair question. The answer is, "to some extent, yes." There are two reasons why the term "to some extent" is being used here.

As explained earlier, the elements of the OECD CLI are economic data of the member nations. The data releases are often delayed and may not make it into the calculation of the OECD CLI in time for first release. The resulting possibility of revisions in the CLI time series was alluded to earlier in the text. If the data sets are often not available on time, then it is even more difficult to get them beforehand. This is the first reason.

The second reason is that the exact computational algorithm of the CLI is complex. Even if we know every data point that goes into the computation, we cannot make accurate predictions unless we know exactly how each data point fits into the equations. Unless we are able to obtain the exact computational software used by the OECD, the task is close to impossible.

Still, whether the new CLI figure will come out weaker or stronger than a month before depends on the changes in each constituent data point, and some of the constituent data can be attained before their official release. This is the reason why we can make predictions "to some extent."

To offer a few examples, if we limit our discussion to the G7 OECD CLI, the US, which has approximately 50% weight in the indicator as seen in Table 1.1, has seven elements (as of February 2016)—Housing

Starts, Durable Goods New Orders, NY Stock Index, Consumer Sentiment, Weekly Hours of Work, ISMPMI (to be discussed later), and Long-term Short-term Interest Rate Spread—and all of these can most certainly be assessed before the official release date of the OECD CLI.

Japan, which has the second largest weight, has elements such as the Inventory to Shipment Ratio, Import/Export Ratio, Loans/Deposits Ratio, Monthly Overtime Hours, Dwelling Started, Share Price Index, Interest Rate Spread, and Small Business Survey. Out of these, at least the Share Price Index and Interest Rate Spread are readily available to the public long before the OECD release date. The case is the same with the other G7 members. If these data points come out significantly "stronger" or "weaker" than the numbers from the month before, we can likely make assumptions before their official release that the next OECD CLI numbers may turn up or down.

The last salient point to be raised is a repeat of what we saw in the last section and has to do with the fact that the OECD CLI was originally developed to forecast peaks and troughs of the economy, but asset prices, whether equities or commodities, while reflecting economic conditions, do not move because of the economy alone.

To be more precise, over a long period of time, equity markets move largely in unison with the economy, but in the shorter term, often the market movements are more affected by factors outside of economic conditions (e.g., policy changes, wars, supply-demand imbalance). It cannot be emphasized enough that the OECD CLI is suitable for forecasting the direction of the Japanese equity market over an extended period of time but not for short-term fluctuations.

The 72% win ratio of the G7 OECD CLI (last reminder, using the deviation from the 1-year moving average of the original time series) in predicting the direction of the Japanese equity market is probably a satisfactory figure for any macroeconomic indicator. The pathway to "enormous wealth" may be considered well paved by this indicator alone, and readers may wish to close this book at this point. In other words, if a reader does not require a return above what the OECD CLI may be able to provide, the remainder of this book may be considered "noise."

Simultaneously, however, if we wish to pursue better returns or a higher probability of winning odds, what the 72% win ratio tells us is that sometimes we may need to bet against the signals of the OECD CLI. To make such judgments, we need a better understanding of the market, which includes not only economic conditions but also information about elements outside of the economy, such as policy implications, wars, natural disasters, and seasonality. To quantify the influence of these elements is clearly not an easy task.

In the future, perhaps AI can solve this problem, but at present, we can only resort to experience in the market and introspection into human nature. The remainder of this book will be dedicated to providing and studying potentially valuable indicators and factors, on top of the OECD CLI, for better understanding of and benefiting from the Japanese equity market.

Economy Watchers' DI

There are myriad macroeconomic indicators, and even casual readers must have heard somewhere in news reports such terms as "BoJ Tankan," "Preliminary GDP," "US Unemployment Statistics," and "Manufacturing PMI." I have not tested the validity of all of the available macroeconomic indicators against the Japanese equity market. I have, however, tested those commonly believed to be important. The conclusion reached is that most of those indicators were more or less unqualified as leading indicators of the Japanese equity market.

In the last couple of sections, the validity of the OECD CLI was argued for extensively (for simplicity, henceforth the term "OECD CLI" will be used to mean the "deviation from the 1-year moving average of the G7 OECD CLI"). In this section, I would like to introduce another macroeconomic indicator that has the promise of becoming as good as or even better than the OECD CLI. That macroeconomic indicator is the Economy Watchers' DI.

The Economy Watchers' DI (Diffusion Index) is the resultant data points and time series of the monthly Economy Watchers' Survey conducted by the Japanese Cabinet Office. The details of the survey can be found on the Cabinet Office homepage (http://www.cao.go.jp/index-e.html), but put simply, the DI is the collection of answers from 2,500 individuals in position to observe economic activities such as household, industrial, and employment.

The survey is conducted every month from the 25th to the month's end, and the results are made public from the 8th to the 12th of the following month. The questions asked in the survey are simple: pick the best answers from "Good," "Fair," "Neutral," "Poor," and "Bad" about (1) the current state of the economy compared with three months before and (2) the expected future state of the economy two to three months ahead. Answers come with points weighted by the number of eligible answers and are summed in the end to calculate the final scores. The time series "Headline" and "Outlook" are thus generated.

As the effectiveness of the OECD CLI comes alive not from the original time series but from its deviation from the 1-year moving average, it is interesting to note that the Economy Watchers' DI also measures the "change" from 3 months before and to 2 to 3 months ahead. For the Economy Watchers' DI to have forecasting power comparative to the OECD CLI, however, the raw time series needs to be modified, according to backtested results.

The first modification needed is seasonality adjustment, which generally refers to a statistical procedure to eliminate seasonality from time series data. For example, if we look at retail numbers, we will not be surprised to see retail business pick up during the Christmas season. If we ignore the seasonality factor, it looks as though the whole economy has picked up suddenly. If we really wish to know the state of the economy, rather than comparing November numbers to December numbers, we should instead compare December numbers this year with December numbers the year before.

Although a few different statistical methods exist for seasonality adjustment, the Cabinet Office, fortunately, already provides seasonally adjusted "Headline" and "Outlook" time series. The actual computational method used for seasonality adjustment is within the realm of statistics explained in the aforementioned Cabinet Office homepage. One issue we may note, however, is that the historical validity of the Economy Watchers' DI cannot be examined directly from the raw seasonally adjusted time series. This is because the seasonality adjustment is performed once a year and at that time, the whole historical time series gets modified.

If the whole historical time series gets modified every year, then the historical backtest appears to become meaningless, because what we see today as history was not what we saw as history when it was released in earlier years.

The Cabinet Office, well aware of this issue, examined the difference between the "original" seasonally adjusted time series and the time series after annual modifications. The conclusion was that the difference between the two was not of large magnitude. Thus, though perhaps not ideal, using the historical seasonally adjusted time series (after modification) should not render the backtest as "meaningless" as initially thought. The use of the seasonally adjusted time series, however, is still not enough to generate decent returns when trading TOPIX, by repeating "buy" when the signal turns up from the month before and "sell" when the signal turns down (although the results were superior to using the raw seasonally unadjusted time series data). In order to enhance the effectiveness of the Economy Watchers' DI as a leading indicator, we need to further tweak the methodology employed.

The tweaking needed is to add the predetermined "threshold value" or the "degree" to which the signal turns up or down from the month earlier. Both "Headline" and "Outlook" seasonally adjusted DIs are available from August 2001 onward, with numbers swinging from 20 to 60. To what degree does the number need to change (or what threshold value needs to be set) to function as an effective leading indicator? After some trial and error, the optimal degree or the threshold value has turned out to be somewhere between 1 and 2.

After all these alterations, what sort of return can we expect out of the Economy Watchers' DI? Assuming we purchased and sold TOPIX according to the Economy Watchers' DI signals, as we did with the OECD CLI, and setting "the threshold value" to be 1.5, since August 2001, the resultant cumulative return up to August 2016 is 692%, with a "win ratio" of 70%. During the same period, the OECD CLI would have given us the cumulative return of 468% with the "win ratio" of 67%.

The performance differentials may tempt us to do away with the OECD CLI and stick to the Economy Watchers' DI going forward. There are, however, arguments in favor of the OECD CLI.

First, the Economy Watchers' DI has not withstood the test of time, unlike the OECD CLI. Due to the "adjustments" and "tweaking" added to the raw time series, the backtest results were superior, but whether these "adjustments" and "tweaking" will continue to function in the future is still a question.

Second, the economical plausibility of the Economy Watchers' DI can easily be challenged. While the OECD CLI is a computational product of the collection of economic data from the member nations, the Economy Watchers' DI stems from the collection of opinions or impressions by ordinary citizens. Common sense tells us that objective economic data such as the Manufacturing PMI and Durable Goods New Orders have more validity than the opinions of ordinary folks.

Additionally, as mentioned earlier, the OECD CLI is an ever-changing scientific tool, subject to revisions and improvements by the OECD, according to the nature of ever-changing markets. This is in contrast with the Economy Watchers' DI, which follows a prefixed formula. In fact, in the fifteen years up to August 2016, the Economy Watchers' DI recorded 43 inflection points of the economy, while the OECD CLI recorded only 31 in the last 25 years. Forty-three alterations of the state of the economy in the 15-year period seems a little too many. Thus, in this regard also, the OECD CLI may have an edge over the Economy Watchers' DI in reflecting the economic reality.

In what area, then, does the Economy Watchers' DI appear superior to the OECD CLI, apart from the aforementioned track record? For one, we need not be bothered by the monthly revisions. Although we need to cope with the yearly seasonality adjustments in the Economy Watchers' DI, the raw unadjusted time series are left alone to be examined at any time.

Second, the time lag is limited in the Economy Watchers' DI. The OECD CLI raw data comes out with a delay after the fact of about a month and ten days, but the delay is only about a week for the Economy Watchers' DI. Presumably, therefore, the Economy Watchers' DI is more likely to better reflect the "current" state of the economy.

Lastly, the Economy Watchers' DI is easier to understand. While each of the components of the OECD CLI is clearly stated and assessed, the calculation of the end result is out of our reach due to the complex computational methodology—we have no choice but to trust the OECD. In the Economy Watchers' DI, though we still have to trust the Cabinet Office, the survey results are transparent and their veracity can easily be checked.

ISMPMI

As a more traditional macro indicator, the ISMPMI (Institute of Supply Management Purchasing Managers Index) deserves to be highlighted. The indicator is a result of the survey of purchasing managers from over 400 companies based in the US, and therefore, the approach is similar to that of the Economy Watchers' DI. Additionally, the data points released are seasonally adjusted numbers, subject to change annually at the beginning of each year. The ISMPMI is similar to the Economy Watchers' DI in this regard, as well.

The Institute of Supply Management (ISM) is also aware of a discrepancy between the original seasonally adjusted time series and annually adjusted time series. The discrepancy, however, is too small to be material, according to the ISM.

The survey is conducted in five categories—orders received, production, employment, supply, and inventory—and the answers are tallied based on a comparison with those of the previous month (plus or minus), weighted, and seasonally adjusted. The final number appears as a percentage, with 50% being neutral, above 50% indicating improvement in sentiment, and below 50% suggesting deteriorating conditions.

The monthly tallies are collected for manufacturers and non-manufacturers separately, with the manufacturing data customarily disclosed on the first business day and non-manufacturing data on the third business day of the month. Approximately 90% of the US economy is due to the non-manufacturing sector, but what carries more significance for the Japanese equity market is the manufacturing data (hence, for simplicity, the ISMPMI in the text will stand for the ISM manufacturing PMI going forward).

Some of the well-known economists have considered the ISMPMI to be one of the more important US economic indicators, former Fed chairman Alan Greenspan among them. As mentioned earlier, one of the US OECD CLI components is also the ISMPMI.

As with the OECD CLI and many other economic indicators, the ISMPMI data is released monthly, but its time series generally displays more frequent ups and downs than the OECD CLI. What we see is the ISMPMI rising and falling from month to month, often drifting in one direction or another (in other words, the ISMPMI time series is volatile).

Even though the ISMPMI is a component time series of the OECD CLI, the return generated by buying and selling TOPIX by this indicator is not impressive. The backtest result since the early 1990s gives us a win ratio of about 50%. One of the reasons for this poor win ratio is due to the high volatility of this indicator.

Table 1.4 is the result of using the 3-month moving average of this indicator as the signal for buying and selling TOPIX from July 31, 1990, to March 31, 2017. The 3-month moving average is to smooth out the high volatility. If the 3-month moving average rises relative to the 3-month

TABLE 1.4 Trading TOPIX by ISMPMI

Cumulative Return	Average Return	Stdev	Win Ratio
406.40%	3.20%	13.60%	59.40%

Sources: ISM, TSE

TABLE 1.5 TOPIX returns after significant fall of ISMPMI

	1W After	1M After	3M After
Average	−1.50%	−3.00%	−4.90%
Median	−0.80%	−0.90%	−6.60%
Maximum	3.40%	3.80%	16.30%
Minimum	−10.10%	−27.90%	−21.30%
Win Ratio	29.20%	34.80%	30.40%

Sources: ISM, TSE

moving average the month before, then the signal is a "buy," and if it falls, a "sell."

The win ratio has improved, but still the overall results are greatly inferior to those of the OECD CLI (other moving averages were also tested, but the results were worse). For the Japanese equity market, therefore, the usefulness of the ISMPMI is not due to its ability to provide inflection points for the market. For that purpose, we should stick to the OECD CLI or Economy Watchers' DI. Why are we talking about the ISMPMI at all then?

Table 1.5 lists the returns of TOPIX 1 week, 1 month, and 3 months after the ISMPMI fell more than 5% relative to the ISMPMI the month before. The samples were collected since 1990.

We see that the returns lean strongly toward negative, although not always. What it says is that whenever the ISMPMI falls significantly, it is a sign that the US economy has suffered a setback, and we should at least be cautious or outright bearish on Japanese equities.

Incidentally and interestingly, sudden improvement of the ISMPMI does not necessarily lead to strong TOPIX returns. The truism that market volatility is more often due to negative surprises than positive ones may be understood from this fact alone. Namely, positive surprises, whether they are from the ISMPMI or other sources, do not on average jumpstart the equity market.

Once again, the equity market is a mirror of human psychology as well as the economy. When we sense a looming danger, what we do immediately is try to dodge it. Only after the apparent danger is gone will we try to identify what the exact danger was. What about when we receive a good omen? Probably we will try to check whether it is true first before taking an appropriate action. Humans are basically cautious creatures, and investment behavior directly reflects human nature.

Seasonality

It is well known that the stock market possesses certain seasonality. The proverb "Sell in May" came from America, and so did the "Halloween Effect." The Japanese equity market is no exception. We can in fact show that by repeating a simple strategy of selling TOPIX on May 1 of each year and buying it back on November 1 of the same year, we could have, at least historically, achieved an appreciable return.

For example, let us assume that from 1990, we sold TOPIX on May 1 and bought it back on November 1. In this case, the cumulative return achieved by November 1, 2017, would have been 453%, with a win ratio of 66% (Table 1.6). The cumulative return is well below that of the OECD CLI, but the win ratio is only a few percentage points below.

If seasonality works so well, what if economic signals go against seasonality? The answer is that economic indicators such as the OECD CLI more often than not dominate seasonality. Yet one interesting fact regarding this matter is that whether by coincidence or by design, market inflection points signaled by economic indicators, particularly by the OECD CLI, tend to be in line with those indicated by seasonality.

Why seasonality exists in the equity market is an often-asked question. A quick answer might be that the economy itself may inherently possess certain seasonality. Perhaps another explanation is the mass mentality. The equity market is similar to a beauty pageant. If everyone believes that the equity market will go higher, it will, and if everyone believes otherwise, it will fall. Needless to say, there is always a seller for every buyer, and thus their numbers are equal. What is meant here is the level of the market; in other words, if everyone agrees that

TABLE 1.6 "Sell in May" and TOPIX returns

	Return	Cumulative Return	Win Ratio
Sell in May	110.30%	117.70%	66.70%
Buy in Nov	129.70%	154.40%	65.40%
Total	240.10%	453.70%	66.00%

Source: TSE

the market should be at 100, then the market will be at that level, and if everyone believes that the market should be 90, then the market will fall to that level. Whatever the case may be, if everyone thinks that the market will fall in May, then the market will be sold. The end result is that of a self-fulfilled prophecy. The same can be said of November, and to say that this is the reason for seasonality may have some plausibility.

Another explanation for seasonality is that many hedge funds in the US and Europe have year-end in September and October, and hence there is new money inflow into the equity market in November. This explanation may be questionable, as seasonality existed long before hedge funds began to exert considerable force.

Also questionable is a theory that since US companies generally pay bonuses at the end of January, the inflow of the new money thus generated lasts until May. Foreign investors did not become dominant in the Japanese equity market until the 1990s. This theory, therefore, cannot explain the seasonality before 1990.

Figure 1.2 compares the average monthly Nikkei 225 returns since 1980 and 2004. Although the general seasonality patterns are similar, quite a few differences are observed in the monthly returns, most notably for January, May, and June.

Figure 1.3 looks at the "win ratio" of each month, where again, the "win ratio" measures the ratio of positive returns against the total number of returns. The overall patterns are once again similar, but we see large differences for February, June, August, and September.

Both figures confirm the existence of seasonality, but they also tell us that depending upon the time span, the degree of seasonality can differ appreciably. In fact, if we limit the time span to the last ten years, the May win ratio rises to 60%. Looking more closely at the difference between

FIGURE 1.2 Average Nikkei 225 monthly returns

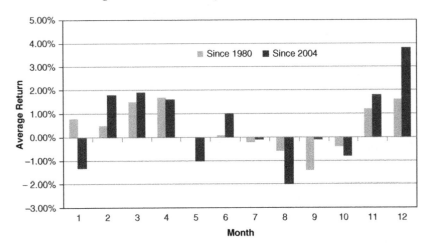

Source: FRED

FIGURE 1.3 Monthly Nikkei 225 "Win Ratio"

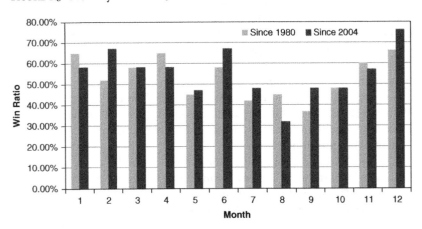

Source: FRED

the last 25 and 10 years, we see the elements of "accident" skewing the landscape. Take, for example, 2009. The market was orchestrating an impressive rebound out of the mal-effect of the 2007–2008 global financial crisis from March onward. The valuations were at rock-bottom, and investors, with hope of economic recovery and faith in central banks, were scrumming to get their hands on equities once again in May. Another example is 2013's market. Investors were dancing to the tune of "Abenomics" after "Kuroda bazooka" (both explained in later chapters) exploded in April. The rise of the equity market was too much too fast, however, and we saw it come crumbling down on May 23. The market saw a phenomenal decline for the next two months, but the May performance, measured from April 30 to May 31, still was positive.

Two such positive outcomes in ten years would naturally improve the win ratio for the month of May. Whether the "Sell in May" proverb will cease to function going forward remains to be seen.

CHAPTER 2

Policy Impact

I t is no surprise that policy decisions affect the equity market. Tax cuts and fiscal stimuluses are designed to keep the economy afloat and thus give support to the equity market. Likewise, monetary policies, depending on how they are used, work either to lift up or to slow down the equity market. Looking back at history, the creation and demise of the '80s bubble, the "lost 20 years" since the 1990s, the Koizumi bull market of 2005, and the equity market since the introduction of "Abenomics" were all orchestrated in large part by policy decisions. Monetarists believe that the Bank of Japan (BoJ) monetary policies are to blame for the lost 20 years, while traditionalists believe that the blame should be placed on the lack of structural reform in Japan (such as needed pro-growth deregulation of corporate laws and change in taxation codes, change in the immigration policy, etc.). Either way, policy decisions are believed to be the main culprit.

"Policy decisions" discussed in this chapter are not limited to those in Japan. The Japanese equity market reacts sensitively to global economic conditions and is often swayed not only by American policy decisions but also by those of the EU or China. Decisions made by the Federal Reserve Board (the Fed), results of US presidential elections, actions by the European Central Bank (the ECB), and Brexit, just to name a few, have exerted considerable force on the Japanese equity market and will likely continue to do so.

The aim of this chapter is not to analyze in detail or offer a critique on each policy decision. Rather, the aim is to offer observations on the Japanese equity market when significant policy decisions were made, with the hope that investors can use the information in structuring future investment strategies.

What this means is that even if certain policies are important in theory, if they have minimal impact on the Japanese equity market, they will not be discussed in this chapter. Accordingly, we take a phenomenological approach and mainly examine how and why particular policy decisions since Abenomics affected the Japanese equity market.

Abenomics

"Abenomics" is the term coined to denote the set of policy actions aimed at resurrecting the Japanese economy by adopting both monetarist and traditionalist ideas. More precisely, "Abenomics" refers to the set of policies called the "three arrows" advocated by Prime Minister Shinzo Abe: "bold monetary policy," "aggressive fiscal policy," and "growth policy to stimulate private sector investment."

The "bold monetary policy" meant appointing Haruhiko Kuroda, a well-known monetarist, as governor of the BoJ. "Aggressive fiscal policy" meant instituting the immediate fiscal stimulus package of over JPY10 trillion. "Growth policy to stimulate private sector investment" was to be done through deregulations at levels never attempted before.

If my memory serves me, the term "Abenomics" began to circulate around November 2012. Obviously, the term was patterned after "Reaganomics" of the 1980s or "Clintonomics" of the 1990s, both of which were believed to have succeeded in rejuvenating the then-ailing US economy. As seen in the performance of the TOPIX or Nikkei 225, the Japanese stock market, not to mention the entire economy, was also ailing pre-Abenomics.

The Japanese stock market was just about to get out of the wake of the 2008 financial crisis when the Great East Japan Earthquake struck on March 11, 2011. The subsequent Fukushima nuclear accident (to be discussed in a later chapter) and the July 2011 flood in Thailand delivered devastating blows to the Japanese economy and corporate profit.

There isn't much anybody can do when it comes to natural disasters. The truth is, however, that even long before 2011, the Japanese equity market performance lagged that of other nations. One of the reasons was the currency.

The foreign exchange (FX) rate between the US and Japan is historically and closely linked to growths in the monetary base of the two nations, and the growth differentials come from policy differentials of the central banks. In order to resuscitate the economy after 2008, the US central bank (the Fed) engaged in dramatic monetary easing, while Japan's counterpart, the BoJ, comparatively did nothing. The end result was to accelerate monetary base growth in the US, and the strong Japanese yen (JPY) was left uncorrected until 2012 (further discussion is provided below in the "FX and the Japanese Equity Market" section).

Another reason the Japanese equity market performed so poorly pre-2012 was politics. In August 2009, the Democratic Party of Japan won the lower house election by a landslide and gained control. Voters, sick and tired of the volatile stock market and ever-widening divides between socioeconomic classes, said a historical "No" to the Liberal Democratic

Party (LDP) for the first time in a long while. The Democratic Party turned out to be no shining star, however, as it repeated a series of political missteps, not to mention the poor handling of the Great East Japan Earthquake and Fukushima nuclear accident in 2011.

Although plummeting popularity forced then PM Noda of the Democratic Party to officially dismiss the lower house on November 16, 2012, the likelihood of dismissal was already reported widely two days earlier, by November 14. The closing price of the Nikkei 225 on November 14 was JPY8664.73, on the 15th it was JPY8829.72, and on the 16th it surpassed JPY9,000.

Customarily in Japan, we do not see many cases where elections move the equity market in any significant fashion. Even when the Democratic Party of Japan won the historic August 2009 election, the market showed only a small sign of recovery before falling back down. The only memorable exception of the modern era pre-2012 was the September 11, 2005, election, where then PM Koizumi of the LDP dismissed the lower house in August to gain support for his postal privatization agenda.

In 2005, the Nikkei 225, on a moderate recovery path after recording a year-to-date low on April 21, jumped on the news of lower house dismissal on August 11 only to begin further ascent after September 11. Ultimately, the Nikkei 225 rose to a high of 17563.37 on April 7, 2006, which, when calculated from 12098.08 marked on August 10, the day before the lower house dismissal, was a gain of 45.2%.

Of course, anyone can say, "I told you so," once the results are known, and surely we could not have known how much the Nikkei 225 would rise because of the lower house election. Nevertheless, it was not difficult to foresee that the market would rise as a result of PM Koizumi, a staunch reformist, gaining general support from the public.

There were, however, other factors at work in the 2005–2006 bull market. First, as seen in Table 1.3, the G7 economy was beginning to show signs of recovery on July 11, 2005. Recall that the OECD CLI numbers are released about a month and ten days after the fact. In other words, the G7 economy was on the mend by the end of May 2005, and other signs of economic recovery were probably visible even outside of the OECD CLI.

The second factor was the Fed, which, in response to the strength in the US economy, began raising rates almost monthly starting in June 2004. The Japanese counterpart, the BoJ, on the other hand, kept the short-term rates steady. As a result, the interest rate differentials widened between the two nations, which contributed to weakening the Japanese currency against the US dollar. A weaker Japanese yen is generally conducive to a stronger Japanese equity market.

Thus, even without the lower house election, it would not have been difficult to imagine the Japanese equity market climbing to a certain level. The hopes for the Koizumi reform, however, most likely added a few more percentage points to that level.

Returning to 2012, after the dismissal of the lower house on November 16, the Japanese equity market remained in an upward trajectory, with the Nikkei 225 marking 9828.88 the day after the lopsided victory by the LDP in the election. Calculated from November 14, just a month before, the gain was over 13%.

From the high unfavorable rating of the Democratic Party of Japan, it was clear from the start that the election would be a disaster for the incumbents. In addition, Shinzo Abe of the LDP, who was slated to be the next PM, had been an advocate of proactive fiscal spending and monetary easing aimed at rejuvenating the Japanese economy. As the stock market is a mirror of investor sentiment, predicting a positive outcome was easy when the Democratic Party, long viewed as something of a pariah, lost the election by a wide margin, and also the birth of the pro-growth Abe cabinet spelled a bull market in anyone's eyes.

We readily speak of the "Abenomics market," but the definition of it is not all that clear. In fact, the Abenomics market has had several peaks. The Nikkei 225 suggests that the first peak was reached on May 22, 2013, after a gain of 73% from November 16, 2012, in about a six-month period.

Once again, though, the election was not the only cause of the phenomenal bull market that began in November 2012. One contributing factor was seasonality. As seen in Table 1.6 in the "Seasonality" section in Chapter 1, simply buying TOPIX in November and selling it in May of every year historically generates the 66% probability of attaining a positive return. But perhaps something more significant than seasonality was going on at the time. Referring to Table 1.3 tells us that the world witnessed the rebound of the G7 economy on November 9, 2012. Hence, the rapid rise of the Japanese equity market was due to three major factors: the election, seasonality, and the recovery of the G7 economy.

The supporting evidence of the "tri-factor" conjecture comes from the stock markets of other nations. The fact of the matter is that the equity markets in the US, UK, Germany, Hong Kong, and other major nations were all beginning to rebound from mid-November 2012.

BoJ and Kuroda Bazooka

The first of the "three arrows" being "bold monetary policy," it was the Bank of Japan (BoJ) that launched the initial projectile of Abenomics. On March 20, 2013, Haruhiko Kuroda, the former head of Asia Development Bank, was appointed the 31st governor of the BoJ, replacing Masaaki Shirakawa.

From his career and his views expressed even before appointment, Kuroda came with a reputation as a proactive monetarist. Since his becoming the governor was largely expected, however, the appointment generated little surprise, and although the Nikkei 225 rose moderately the following day, it failed to perform in any impressive manner afterward.

The Nikkei 225 had risen 40% already from November 16, 2012, to March 20, 2013, and investors were growing nervous about how much more upside they could expect out of the Japanese equity market. The reasons for the nervousness came from abroad: the Cypriot financial crisis and the apparent slowdown in the US economy.

The Cypriot financial crisis of 2013 stemmed from the series of Euro crises that had dogged the world economy since the 2007–2008 global financial crisis, and for most market observers, it was like a UFO suddenly appearing on the radar screen. Because Cyprus's GDP was a mere 0.2% of the EU, the financial trouble in the nation seemed insignificant, to say the least. The concern over the Cypriot financial crisis, however, was not the size of the nation's GDP but its backdrop.

Put simply, financially troubled Cyprus was receiving aid from the EU in return for fiscal austerity and discipline. But the Cypriot citizens rebelled against the austerity measures imposed, and the government could no longer keep the promises it had made to the EU.

If the issue had been limited to Cyprus, the market probably would have shrugged off the Cypriot crisis. What shook the market was a fear that similar situations would spread like wildfire to other EU nations, nations with much larger GDPs, that were also on the receiving end of the financial support. These nations included Greece, Portugal, Spain, and even Italy. If the general public in these countries rejected the tough EU measures, either the nations would have had to leave the union, or the EU authority would have had to give up on financial discipline. In other words, the market feared the demise of the European Union.

In the end, with the announcement of new relief measures from the EU on March 25, the smoldering embers of the Cypriot crisis died out.

Still, the probability of similar incidents popping up elsewhere in the EU community was by no means nil, and for investors, visibility remained quite poor. In a case such as this, it is probably best either to stay away from equities or reduce equity holding until visibility becomes less opaque. Usually, it will not be too late to jump back into equities when the solution to the problem becomes well defined.

As for the US economy, the first sign of deterioration showed itself in the ISMPMI, which fell to 51.3, well below consensus expectation and down 5.4% from the previous month. The size of the decline ranked within the top 20 in the past quarter century.

As noted in the "ISMPMI" section in Chapter 1, when the ISMPMI drops by a significant amount, the Japanese equity market performance becomes generally weak. At this time, however, not too many investors had become "sellers." The reason was that the BoJ was expected to release the first policy statement after Kuroda's appointment, on April 4, and the market was holding its breath in anticipation.

Indeed, on April 4, 2013, the Kuroda-led BoJ announced a level of quantitative easing unparalleled by anything in the past. The policy, called "monetary easing of a different dimension" by Governor Kuroda himself, was to set a 2% inflation target, and to achieve this goal within two years, the government was to double the monetary base (increase of JPY60 trillion – JPY70 trillion per annum).

The policy was to reverse Japan's inferior position against the US in monetary base growth, and although the "achievability" came into immediate question, the policy was enough to convince the market of the BoJ's commitment to reignite Japan's ailing economy. The Nikkei 225, as a result, rose 2.2% on the very day of the announcement and went on to rise 24% by May 22, 2013.

The impressive performance of the Nikkei 225 added a layer of polish on the armor of Haruhiko Kuroda as a consummate monetarist. It proved that, even without addressing structural impediments such as Japan's demography, monetary easing had the force to push up the Japanese equity market, albeit in the short term. In addition, the strength of the equity market showed that when faced with a policy move of this magnitude, the worries over EU finance or the concerns over the sudden slowdown of the US economy were very much powerless.

As the equity market mirrors human psyche, guessing that the BoJ's unprecedented monetary easing would blow away the concerns over

FIGURE 2.1 Nikkei 225 (10/31/2012–7/31/2013).

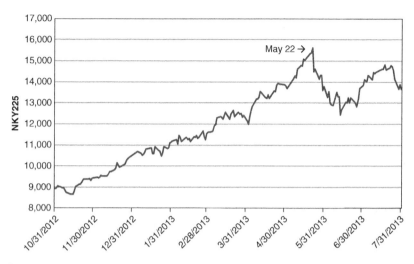

Source: FRED

Europe and America at least in the near term would not have been difficult. Indeed, investors were willing to bet on this very possibility. The first Abenomics bull market peaked on May 22, 2013. On May 23, the Nikkei 225 plummeted 7.3% and by June 13, saw a decline of over 20% (Figure 2.1). The 7.3% drop in a day ranks sixth measured from 1989, and if we ignore the records in October 2008 (the global financial crisis) and March 2011 (the Great East Japan Earthquake), ranks first.

Why did the Japanese equity market experience a correction of this severity despite the unparalleled BoJ monetary easing? We could perhaps pinpoint a few causes, but to predict the timing and magnitude of the correction was nearly impossible. This is because the direct culprit behind the market drop was the congressional testimony by then Fed Chairman Ben Bernanke on May 22 (US local time).

In his testimony, Ben Bernanke alluded to "tapering" (reduction of monetary easing) for the first time, suggesting the possibility of a US central bank policy moving from monetary easing to effective tightening. Since the 2007–2008 global financial crisis, the US as well as global financial markets had largely been supported by the Fed's loose monetary policy. Bernanke's suggestion of a change in this policy stance, therefore, sent shockwaves across the global equity markets, and Japan did not escape the negative impact.

There are other reasons why the Japanese equity market's fall was particularly pronounced, however. First, we must look at technical indicators, which are typically used to judge if the market is overbought or oversold. The RSI, Bollinger Band, and Toraku ratios are just a few examples of commonly used technical indicators. (See the section "Valuations and Technical Indicators" in Chapter 4.)

As of May 22, almost all technical indicators were flashing "overbought" or "overheat" signs. A word of caution is that even when these indicators suggest "overbought" or "oversold" conditions, the market does not necessarily experience a meaningful correction. This time, however, the market actually did.

The bet on the BoJ monetary easing was a bet on hopes. No one knew how much actual impact the BoJ's policy move would generate on the Japanese economy. A bull market bought on hopes alone usually does not last long. In this regard, monetary easing works as a shot in the arm but not as a permanent remedy.

By the end of March, the deceleration of the US economy was evident, as discussed earlier. Not only the ISMPMI but also housing starts and durable goods new orders were signaling the slowdown. The Japanese long yield (yield of the long-term bond) nevertheless continued to rise. Rising yields in the face of a slowing economy are called "a bad interest rate increase," and are often signs of market turmoil. During the days preceding May 22, we witnessed ominous escalation of the interest rates.

Perhaps the sign that most accurately foretold the collapse of the equity market on May 23 was the futures cash arbitrage position (influence of futures on cash is discussed in Chapter 3, "Topics Derivatives").

Futures arbitragers take up a section on the trading floor and play an important role in the equity market. Futures and common equities (called cash equities) are uniquely related by a simple mathematical formula, and when either one breaks away from the formula, the event is called an arbitrage opportunity, a chance to generate risk-free profit. In a bull market, futures tend to be bought and thus tend to rise above appropriate cash levels, creating arbitrage opportunities (the opposite takes place in a bear market).

When an arbitrage opportunity is created in a bull market, what arbitragers do is to sell futures and buy back cash. By definition, the futures price at expiry must match the cash price at that time. Arbitragers take advantage of this relationship and take the spread between futures and cash before expiry.

Since arbitragers typically sell futures and buy cash, the act naturally creates the cash arbitrage position. On May 22, the futures cash arbitrage position (Nikkei 225 and TOPIX combined) was at a record high, and when compared with the levels of the Nikkei 225 and TOPIX, did not look reasonable. This should have rung the alarm if nothing else did so. When futures are sold, arbitragers must sell cash to close their positions. There is little doubt that the arbitragers' action contributed to the market collapse of May 23, as the cash arbitrage position saw a phenomenal decrease on that day.

Abenomics Market II

While there are differing views on the time period, if we consider the first Abenomics market to have begun in mid-November 2012 and ended on May 22, 2013, its lifespan was only about six months long. And here, we simply define the first Abenomics market to be during that six-month period.

In fact, after falling 3200 points (20%) from 15627.26 on May 22 to 12445.38 on June 23, the Nikkei 225 continued its undulating and lackluster performance until the end of November, where it finally gained back what it lost after May 22. Afterward, the index largely remained in its upward trajectory until December 30 that year, where it recorded 16291.31 at close.

Since the Nikkei 225 closed the previous year at 10395.18, the gain in 2013 was 56.7%, a respectable return despite the mediocre second half. When we consider the gain of 50% by May 22, however, we see no problem in regarding the first Abenomics market ending on that date.

As a side note, the strong December 2013 market is largely due to seasonality and the weaker yen. The weak yen domestically was due to the policy rumor that the BoJ might conduct additional easing and also that the GPIF (Government Pension Investment Fund) might announce an asset allocation change more favorable to equities. Overseas, the threat was the commencement of tapering (effective monetary tightening) by the Fed, which was also conducive to a weaker Japanese currency.

We might add, however, that tapering could have been a double-edged sword, as noted in the previous section. If tapering had been viewed as too much too soon by investors, it would have been a negative factor: the Japanese yen would have been bought and the equity market would have been sold.

The Abenomics market looked as though it was catching a second breath in December 2013, but the looming retirement of Ben Bernanke and the appointment of Janet Yellen as the new Fed chair apparently did not sit well with investors. The Japanese equity market consequently began 2014 with another big plunge.

In January 2014, the new Fed chair, Janet Yellen, initiated "tapering" as expected. The announced stance was propitiatory such that any future tapering would be done at pedestrian pace. The market did not like the move, nevertheless.

What served as the main trigger was not certain—the change of guard at the Fed, commencement of tapering, or yet another factor—but the January ISMPMI, released at the beginning of February, showed a sudden drop in the US economic activity once again. The already weak January equity market was broadsided and went into a tailspin.

If a few words could describe the force that moved the 2014 Japanese equity market, perhaps "worsening of the global economy" best serves the purpose. As seen in Table 1.3, and as epitomized by the sudden decline in the ISMPMI, the deterioration of the G7 economy was clear from January of that year, and we had to wait until November 2014 (the OECD CLI number was released in January 2015) to see clear signs of recovery.

The OECD CLI aside, the Japanese equity market, indexed by the Nikkei 225 (or TOPIX) continued to fluctuate as usual until June and began to rise slowly afterward. In the background were Japan's consumption tax (VAT) hike and surprising strength in the US economy.

On April 1, 2014, Japan's consumption tax was raised from 5% to 8%, and if we judge from the Nikkei 225 moves, its news value, at least, was negative. By June, however, consumer behavior showed that the negative impact of the consumption tax hike might not be as large as initially had been believed (the impact of consumption tax hikes will be discussed later). As for the US economy, the ISMPMI rebounded after the collapse in January and continued to ascend from February on, rising sharply in August. A strong US economy usually results in a weaker Japanese currency, which is generally supportive of the Japanese equity market.

As discussed in the previous chapter, however, the ISMPMI is not necessarily an effective inflection point indicator for Japanese equities. During the time, between February and August, where the ISMPMI was on an upward track, the OECD CLI and Economy Watchers' DI were in a downward spiral, indicating further weakening of the global economy. The September ISMPMI took a nosedive, German industrial production turned sour, the IMF revised down the global economic growth prospect, and all these contributed to a sharp deterioration of the global equity market. The technically "oversold" market subsequently responded with a small bounce, but to compound the problem, the Fed announced the end of QE (quantitative easing), as planned, on October 29.

The fire of uncertainty engulfed the market, as undoubtedly the next step for the Fed would be an interest rate hike. In the following few days, what rescued the global market sentiment, albeit temporarily, was none other than Japan.

The second Abenomics market began on October 31, 2014. On this day, the BoJ, betraying most market expectations, announced additional large-scale QE. The point of the QE was to augment the monetary base by JPY80 trillion per annum through increased purchase of treasury bonds, exchange traded funds (ETFs), and real estate investment trusts (REITs). In no time, the news that the central bank of Japan, responsible for the monetary policy of the third largest economy in the world, was expanding the scale of the historical monetary easing shot through the world's financial markets like a bolt out of the blue. The so-called second Kuroda bazooka yanked down the Japanese yen, and the Nikkei 225 jumped 4.8% in a single day.

As discussed in the "OECD CLI" section in Chapter 1, however, the BoJ was not the sole driver of the Nikkei 225's sharp rise. On the same day, the GPIF announced the historical asset allocation change, moving equity weight from the previous 24% to 50% (25% foreign equities, 25% domestic equities). The change in asset allocation, officially called "basic portfolio review," was not to happen overnight, but the news value of the change from the GPIF, the largest government pension fund in the world, was enough to rekindle the enthusiasm of equity investors domestic and abroad.

Theories and speculations abounded regarding the BoJ and GPIF's moving on the same day to help out the Japanese equity market. One popular theory had to do with the planned October 2015 VAT hike expected to be made official in November 2014. "BoJ and GPIF to neutralize the negative policy impact of VAT hike" was among the headlines we read at the time, as if it were a fact.

The BoJ and GPIF immediately denied such collaboration and insisted that the timing was only an accident. We may never find out the truth, but on November 18, PM Shinzo Abe announced the postponement of the next VAT hike, thereby negating the BoJ-GPIF-VAT theory. What the postponement revealed was that the government, BoJ, and GPIF all shared the same concern over the state of the Japanese economy.

Indeed, the VAT postponement announcement had a positive effect on the Nikkei 225. The news of the postponement, the additional QE, and the GPIF portfolio review altogether propelled the Japanese equity market to higher levels. An equity market helped by policy moves can only remain afloat when accompanied by a solid recovery in the economy, however. As noted earlier, the G7 OECD CLI was already showing a sign of recovery by November, but the revelation of it had to wait until January 2015.

Whether due to the global economic deterioration that had lasted nine months or some other supply-demand issues, crude oil prices began to fall precipitously in early November. The Russian ruble was sold off (the Russian economy was closely tied to oil price), along with the currencies of many developing nations. In December, as rumors of another currency crisis spread, the Japanese yen was bought as a safe haven, and Japanese equities suffered a major setback.

Among the Japanese companies whose share prices were negatively correlated with the crude oil price at that time were ANA, Bridgestone, and Oriental Land, the companies that should benefit from falling fuel prices. Among the companies whose share prices were positively correlated were INPEX and wholesale firms (trading companies). Had we bought ANA and Bridgestone stocks and shorted INPEX or trading firm shares, as the oil prices came tumbling down, the trade would have been quite profitable.

The year 2015 opened with another blow to Japanese equities, as the December ISMPMI ushered in a sign of further disappointment in the US economy. For two consecutive years, Japanese equities suffered a major decline at the beginning of the new year. While all the signs pointed to yet another miserable January, what saved the market was the ECB, as the European Central Bank announced the first QE on January 22.

Incidentally, the Japanese yen fell against the Euro, responding to the disclosure of QE by the ECB at the time. Since the growth of the European monetary base was to accelerate against that of Japan, the expectation was that the yen should rise against the Euro. The reality, however, was that the market turned "risk-on," as the move by the ECB was viewed positively, and the yen was sold as a result. This might be a perfect example that predicting currency movements is not straightforward.

Likely influenced by the ECB's QE, as the OECD CLI illustrates, the global economy gradually began to improve, and along with it, the Japanese equity market. The rising trend ultimately lasted until August 2015. The period between November 2014 and August 2015, thus, may be aptly called Abenomics Market II.

GPIF

In the second Abenomics market, one particular "incident" deserves special attention, as it eloquently reveals the influence of the media on the market. The "incident" affected the market in relation to the aforementioned "portfolio review" by the GPIF.

As of end-2014, the total size of the funds managed by the GPIF was JPY141 trillion, according to the GPIF official release. From this, we could assume that close to this amount was managed at the end of October of the same year. Of this amount, 12% had been allocated to domestic equities before the "portfolio review," which amounted to about JPY17 trillion (in reality, the GPIF gives some slack on both sides of the 12%, and thus the calculation of the exact managed amount in JPY is rather meaningless).

After the "review," the domestic equity weight was raised to 25%, as mentioned earlier. In yen terms, this amounts to about JPY35 trillion, which suggested that some JPY18 trillion would flow into the Japanese equity market via purchase by the GPIF. If JPY18 trillion-worth of equities were bought at once, the equity prices would skyrocket, which would put GPIF at risk of owning equities at the top. To avoid this risk, these purchases are usually done in a measured way. The GPIF, on the other hand, could not wait forever to conduct the asset allocation changes. Accordingly, the GPIF began purchasing equities gradually from October 31, 2014 (some market observers argue that the purchase began much earlier).

The total transaction volume in the Tokyo Stock Exchange Section 1 (TSE1) was in the vicinity of JPY1 trillion to JPY2 trillion per day at the time. The inflow of JPY18 trillion, therefore, as long as it was to be segmented, should not have caused the stock market to spike up. Since any big move by a large public pension fund, however, habitually creates followers, the actual impact was probably much larger than the estimated JPY18 trillion inflow.

What these followers would do was to purchase equities likely to be included in the new equity portfolio before the GPIF actually bought them, or, conversely, to sell stocks whose price had already gone up due to excessive expectations. Either way, what needed to be figured out was the criteria the GPIF would use to select stocks for its new portfolio. Since the GPIF is a public pension fund and not a secretive organization, the management policy and selection criteria are readily disclosed in its homepage.

According to the disclosure, as of the end of December 2014, about 90% of domestic equities were managed passively, and the remaining 10% were managed actively by fourteen different outside managers (the details of "passive" and "active" management of funds are discussed in Chapter 3, "Topics Derivatives").

Since the benchmark for the passive portion was mostly TOPIX, it was not difficult to guess that the stocks in the TOPIX index would be purchased according to their respective weights in the index. Furthermore, investors could expect some inflow of funds into JPX400 stocks as well. This is because the JPX400 Index is a "quality" index consisting of stocks with relatively high ROE (return on equity) and operating profit, whose calculation began from January 6, 2014. The GPIF had decided to employ this index as one of its sub-benchmarks, and therefore, at that time, investors could expect some flow of funds from TOPIX stocks to JPX400 stocks.

In actuality, TOPIX had outperformed JPX400 during this period, and thus, the expected impact of the flow of funds was not observed, at least on the index level. Even if investors had examined the situation more closely, by checking the weights of stocks one by one in each index, it would have been questionable whether they could discern anything more than noise. The reason is that another significant factor was at work at the time. That factor was "volatility." We will delve into volatility in later chapters, but for the time being, let us consider volatility to be the simple rate of change of stock prices (or the index).

Going back to the main point, the Nikkei 225, after falling precipitously at the start of the year, had risen some 14% by the end of March, presumably due to the QE by the ECB and recovery in the global economy, in addition to the GPIF portfolio review. When the overall market is strong, those that outperform initially are usually high-beta (or high-volatility) stocks and value stocks. Against the norm, however, outperformers during this "bull" market were low-volatility defensive stocks.

The role of portfolio managers of domestic institutional investors in general is to outperform the benchmark by adjusting their portfolios. In anticipation of the bull market, those who had shifted portfolio weights to high-volatility and value stocks ended up with stocks that underperformed the benchmark as a result. This is the "incident," and the "incident" took place in relation to media reports, or more precisely, media reports and an "accident."

What about the media reports? The outperformance of low-volatility stocks in the first quarter of 2015 was most apparent in the MSCI Japan Minimum Volatility Index (low-volatility index). The media turned a spotlight on this particular index and reported erroneously that the GPIF had poured a large portion of its funds into the constituent stocks.

The MSCI Japan Minimum Volatility Index consisted of about 150 stocks and is a collection of low-volatility names. The GPIF, however, had not or was not going to invest any funds specifically in this particular index or its constituents. According to the GPIF documents at the time, any "low-volatility" stocks it had or was going to purchase were the members of the GIVI Japan Index, made up of over 1,100 stocks. Considering its large constituent number, the GIVI Japan Index could hardly be called a "low-volatility" index. In addition, since only about JPY25 billion were to be invested in this index, the impact on the overall market could not have been material.

Incidentally, the MSCI Japan Minimum Volatility Index is one of the many indices developed, reviewed, and updated by MSCI. These indices are commonly known as "smart beta" indices and, since they typically possess exposure to certain themes or factors, are favored and followed by a broad spectrum of investors.

When we looked at the historical performance of the MSCI Japan Minimum Volatility Index from 2001 onward, there were no occasions where this index had outperformed the MSCI Japan Value Stock Index outside of bear markets. The period from the last quarter of 2014 to the first quarter of 2015 was exceptional, where the outperformance of the MSCI Japan Minimum Volatility Index versus the MSCI Japan Value Stock Index began with the GPIF asset allocation change announcement and continued despite the subsequent bull market.

In a nutshell, although the GPIF did not put any money into the MSCI Japan Minimum Volatility Index, the index outperformance commenced with the GPIF asset allocation announcement and kept on in the first quarter of the following year. This rather rare phenomenon indeed finds its roots in an "accident."

As discussed in the "Abenomics Market II" section above, the Fed, in the FOMC at the end of October 2014, announced the end of QE. The S&P 500 collapsed following the announcement, and with a sharp spike in the VIX (to be explained later), investors around the world made a decision to shift their funds to more defensive (generally low-volatility) stocks. The shift was temporarily halted by the impact of the second BoJ QE in the following days, only to pick up its pace as the oil price and Russian ruble tumbled starting from early November. The reality, therefore, was that although the overall Japanese equity market was lifted by the GPIF asset allocation decision (recall that 90% of domestic equity funds are allocated passively to TOPIX and JPX400 stocks), the bias from global investors was on defensive low-volatility stocks.

If we limit our analysis to domestic retail investors, the misleading media report of the GPIF's investing in low-volatility stocks figuratively prompted a stampede toward low-volatility stocks. What seemed to be a convincing argument that since the GPIF was moving funds out of bonds and into equities, the funds would naturally go to low-volatility or more bond-like equities, also encouraged purchase of low-volatility stocks. In fact, some European banks and insurers, disliking the low-interest rate environment, indeed shifted part of their funds to low-volatility stocks globally, but the level of the shift probably would not have explained the outperformance of low-volatility stocks in the Japanese equity market at the time. If anything, more impactful were risk-parity funds (to be discussed in Chapter 4, "Market Tops and Bottoms"), types of hedge funds that avoid high-volatility stocks.

Whatever the case may be, as long as we trust the disclosed asset allocation and investment policies of the GPIF, there was no evidence that the organization had or would have shifted funds to low-volatility stocks per se. The most plausible explanation, therefore, is that the bull market orchestrated by the GPIF coincided with the global shift into more defensive stocks. In this regard, this was a perfect example of how media reports were skewed by "accident" and how media reports in turn skewed investor behavior.

Corporate Governance

As part of the Abenomics revolution, corporate governance has become one of the most talked-about concepts. Corporate governance, simply stated, is a measure of how well industries abide by law and act responsibly toward shareholders and society.

With the aim of improving Japan's corporate governance, the Financial Services Agency (FSA) took an initiative and published a series of documents in succession (e.g., "Japan's Stewardship Code: Principles for Responsible Institutional Investors," February 2014, later revised in May 2017; and "Japan's Corporate Governance Code: Seeking Sustainable Corporate Growth and Increased Corporate Value over the Mid- to Long-Term," March 2015).

Viewed sarcastically, institutional investors in Japan before these FSA initiatives were acting irresponsibly and Japanese corporations were not able to govern themselves without help from the government. More constructively, the "Stewardship Code" and "Corporate Governance Code" together lit the light of hope that Japanese institutional investors and corporations would finally reach the levels of governance equivalent to their global peers.

Investors like changes. Even if the changes have no substance, if everyone gets on the bandwagon, the market moves. The FSA-sponsored stewardship or corporate governance was by no means "without substance," but when they were introduced, no one was sure what they were or how they worked. Nevertheless, sensing "changes" on the way, investors abroad in particular were on their toes. The next task for them was to somehow translate the "changes" into investment behavior.

What drew their attention were the organizations such as MSCI, S&P 500, and Bloomberg, the providers of various data and indices. These organizations had the knowhow of quantifying corporate governance, an often elusive and nebulous concept at best, and the validity of the knowhow aside, had measures that could be used immediately.

TABLE 2.1 Annual returns of MSCI Japan ESG Leaders Index and MSCI Japan Index

	2008	2009	2010	2011	2012	2013	2014	2015
MSCI Japan ESG Index	−45.1%	9.2%	−0.1%	−20.8%	17.0%	53.9%	8.4%	14.1%
MSCI Japan Index	−43.6%	7.3%	−1.2%	−20.5%	18.8%	51.9%	7.6%	13.8%

Source: MSCI

Examining these measures in their entirety is beyond the scope of this book and is probably meaningless, since all three organizations employ similar methodologies in quantifying corporate governance. Accordingly, to understand corporate governance and its impact on the market, we resort to ESG (environment, social, governance), a more concrete and central concept and, in particular, to the MSCI Japan ESG Leaders Index.

Table 2.1 compares the yearly performance of the MSCI Japan ESG Leaders Index and MSCI Japan Index. The MSCI Japan ESG Leaders Index was developed and is maintained by MSCI, consisting of stocks MSCI considers adhering to the ESG standards. We do not analyze the MSCI selection or rebalance methodology in detail here, but the concept behind the index may be easily understood because the "E" in ESG stands for environment, "S" for social, and "G" for governance.

In "environment," corporations are literally judged by their response to environmental issues. Automakers may be judged by the amount of CO_2 generated by the cars they manufacture, and food companies may be rated by how friendly to the environment they are in processing food. In "social," companies may be scrutinized based on the labor law or contribution to various social causes. In "governance," compliance, the number of independent board members, accounting transparency, and other disclosure levels may come into question.

Quantifying these criteria is obviously not straightforward. Though the methodologies may be similar, the final score is ultimately left to the discretion of each rating organization (MSCI is no exception). As such, the scores need to be taken with a grain of salt.

As a side note, Toshiba, whose very existence has become doubtful due to accounting mishaps, was once regarded as a shining beacon of corporate governance and indeed many rating agencies were bestowing high marks to this corporation. Kobe Steel, whose falsification of company data became public on October 8, 2017, had long been a member of the MSCI Japan ESG Leaders Index. In fact, the list of corporations listed on this index who were later proved guilty of committing malfeasance included top automakers such as Nissan and Suzuki. These examples are reminiscent of Yamaichi Securities, which was receiving a high investment grade by credit rating agencies up until its bankruptcy in November 1997.

With this understanding, let us now go back to Table 2.1. We note immediately the outperformance of the MSCI Japan ESG Leaders Index over the broader MSCI Japan Index, starting from 2013 on. Needless to say, the likely driving factor behind this outperformance was the government's effort to encourage ESG-based investment. As stated earlier, as a part of this effort, the GPIF had signed on to the "Principles for Responsible Investment," the UN-sponsored ESG platform, effectively inviting other institutional investors to follow suit.

The question was whether this would be a temporary phenomenon. In fact, the performance of ESG-based indices has not been particularly impressive since 2016. Also, in the US, the MSCIUSA ESG Index has not performed particularly well against the broader MSCIUSA Index, while in Europe we tend to see the opposite result.

When the street was buzzing with ESG investments, I asked a friend of mine who was working for a major pension fund in the US about whether his organization was practicing any sort of ESG-based investment. The answer was "Not at all." If this was the general stance taken by US institutional investors, the underperformance by the MSCIUSA ESG Index might come as no surprise. The flipside may be that, unlike Japan, corporate governance in the US was already taken for granted so that it was no longer an issue to be reckoned with.

According to the *Nikkei* on October 18, 2017, ESG-related funds around the world amounted to USD23 trillion, which made up about 30% of the total funds invested globally. The report did not specify exactly what was meant by "ESG-related funds," but European pension funds were known to use ESG as the standard of their investment style, and we already noted the trend in Japan. If the stock investment is indeed a beauty contest, and if everyone favors ESG-conscious companies, then the value of these stocks will likely be supported in the future.

BoJ ETF Purchases

ETF purchases by the BoJ began as part of monetary easing (increasing funds flow to the market) in December 2010. Initially, the purchases were limited to TOPIX-linked ETFs, Nikkei 225-linked ETFs, and J-REITs, but as of August 2017, expanded to include JPX400-linked ETFs and ETFs of the "companies progressive on investing in capital and labor." The funds allocated for the purchases were JPY1 trillion per annum at the start, but as of August 2017, increased to JPY6 trillion.

When the BoJ makes ETF purchases, the process is done in several installments, as usual, to reduce the market impact. The actual purchase is executed by management entities (trust banks), and security firms that receive orders from the management entities purchase stocks that make up particular ETFs (e.g., the Nikkei 225 ETF). The stocks purchased are then exchanged via management entities to create the desired ETFs. By this mechanism, the BoJ not only provides funds to the market but also supports the market by indirectly purchasing equities that constitute broad indices.

While there was no official policy announcement, the initial approach taken by the BoJ was to purchase ETFs (or create ETFs) only when the TOPIX at the morning session close fell more than 1% below the close of the previous trading day. This unwritten rule of thumb was later abandoned, and as of August 2017, ETF purchases appeared to be done when TOPIX morning session levels were simply below the close of the previous trading day (but not always).

The question is whether ordinary investors can make a profit taking advantage of ETF purchases by the BoJ. Understanding the pattern that ETFs are purchased when the TOPIX in the morning session falls below the close of the previous trading day, by buying TOPIX or Nikkei 225 futures at the morning close and selling them at the afternoon close, we may seemingly be able to generate a profitable trade. A backtest performed back in April 2011, however, showed that while the trades generated a 56% win ratio, the average return was negative, suggesting that the strategy would have been a failure.

As for J-REITs, since the overall liquidity of the market was small, investors were able to observe a supportive effect of the BoJ purchases. Unfortunately, however, as the timing of the purchases could not be predetermined, investors had to forego the possibility of using J-REIT purchases to our advantage.

Going back to the TOPIX-linked and Nikkei-linked ETFs, an April 2016 backtest generated more positive returns of the aforementioned strategy, probably due to the increase in purchase size by the BoJ. That said, the average returns were still not large, leaving the validity of the trades in doubt.

On a last, separate topic related to BoJ ETF purchases, when the purchase size was expanded to JPY6 trillion per annum, a view that Japanese equities were a "buy" became a dominant one. The logic was that when foreign investors net-bought Japanese equities to the tune of JPY6 trillion, the market skyrocketed, and a similar upsurge in the market should take place with the BoJ purchases. Turning our eyes to what happened to the market, we can see that this logic was wrong. The reality was that after the change in the purchase size, the Japanese equity market largely treaded sideways, only to see a large upside after Donald Trump was elected US president.

Where the logic went wrong was not understanding the purpose of the purchase. When foreign investors buy Japanese equities as a whole, they tend to bid up, anticipating further upside. On the other hand, BoJ ETF purchases, as stated above, are designed to support a falling market. Accordingly, since the BoJ does not bid up the market, the market does not rise the same way as when foreign investors jump into the Japanese equity market.

Negative Interest Rate Policy

The negative interest rate policy (NIRP) introduced by the BoJ in February 2016 was a never-before-tested policy, and as such, examining NIRP in detail has yet to reveal its validity. As to the effects of NIRP, many studies were cited and speculative news reports were ceaseless, but as of now, judging the true effects still seems premature. Nevertheless, the ushering in of NIRP was a historical event that cannot be circumvented when dissecting Abenomics. Here, we discuss the market environment around the time when NIRP became official and introduce a few analyses.

NIRP literally denotes a policy where the central bank sets its official rates to below 0%, but in the case under discussion, it refers to setting to negative the interest earned on the current account deposits of private banks in the BoJ reserve. In the BoJ policy announced in February 2016, negative interest rates were imposed only on portions of the total deposits, in order to lighten the burden on Japan's major banks.

The idea behind NIRP was that since, for depositors, the negative interest rates on their deposits entailed banks' paying the interest rather than receiving it, the private banks would likely take the funds out of the deposits and use them for investments or loans to corporations. Clearly, the policy was yet another part of BoJ's efforts designed to jumpstart the Japanese economy. The BoJ chose February 2016 for the timing of the NIRP announcement, probably for two reasons: the untimely Fed rate hike in December 2015 and the serious slowdown of the global economy that became apparent after the collapse of the Chinese equity market in August 2015.

The introduction of NIRP by the BoJ, which had long adhered to the zero interest rate policy (ZIRP) and twice orchestrated massive QE, was received by the market both as a surprise and, at the same time, as an act of desperation. The equity market was heavily sold off as a result.

Of course, since the BoJ was altering the interest rate, NIRP's influence on government bonds was also tremendous. Government bonds come with various yields according to their time to maturity. The yield distribution from short-term to long-term is called the yield curve, which, by April 2016, flattened to the extent that even the yield on the 10-year bond fell below 0% due to NIRP.

We might wonder why bestowing negative interest on a portion of the current account deposits in the BoJ reserve would push the government bond yields down. Needless to say, since bond yields are inversely proportional to bond prices, falling yields mean rising prices (i.e., bonds are being bought). Thus, banks were buying government bonds with the money they took out of the BoJ reserve.

Initially, the BoJ lowered the interest rate to negative 0.1%, which meant that the banks had to pay a 0.1% interest to the BoJ if they wished to keep their funds in the BoJ reserve. By this measure, even if the bond yields were at 0% or even negative, as long as they were above negative 0.1%, it would be better to buy bonds than to keep the funds deposited. These observations clearly suggest that there was more than one reason for the market selloff after the introduction of NIRP. Indeed, stocks that were most heavily sold at the time were core financial companies such as banks and life insurers.

One of the traditional, important revenue sources for banks is the spread between short-term interest rates and long-term interest rates. Banks borrow money from the street via short-term deposits, paying interest to depositors, and manage the funds via long-term government bonds (thereby earning interest), taking the spread between the two interest rates. The falling long-term yields, therefore, raised concerns over this traditional business model.

Life insurers, on the other hand, typically sign long-term contracts with policy holders and use the paid premiums to invest in government bonds. Here again, the falling long-term yields meant declining profitability for life-insurers. These are the reasons for the wholesale selloff of Japanese banks and life insurers post-introduction of NIRP.

NIRP, viewed as a last-ditch effort by the BoJ to rescue the Japanese economy from the grips of deflation, evidently worked against the Japanese equity market. The BoJ was not the pioneer of NIRP, however, and indeed the predecessors were the Denmark Central Bank in 2012, the ECB and Swiss Central Bank in 2014, and the Swedish Central Bank in 2015. The BoJ must have known of these forerunners, and only after thoroughly studying the "aftereffects," made the giant leap. What then were the aftereffects?

In a sense, these aftereffects are still ongoing, and to depict every one of them is not the purpose of either this chapter or this book. That said, as far as long-term yields are concerned, in both the nations mentioned above and the Euro zone, we saw these yields uniformly falling after the introduction of NIRP.

NIRP in Europe was originally brought in to cope with the recurrent Euro crises in the aftermath of the 2008–2009 global financial collapse. In a crisis situation, money naturally flows to the safe-haven government bonds, so NIRP was probably not the sole culprit behind the fall in long-term yields. Nevertheless, the timing of the fall and introduction of NIRP were largely coincidental, suggesting at least some influence of the policy.

Regarding the equity market, the effect is less obvious, as the recovery took place globally starting in early 2009 without NIRP, and also the ECB QE in January 2015, in particular, had substantial impact. Only the KAX index appeared to show a strong response immediately following the introduction of NIRP in Denmark, but the dominant factor might be Novo Nordisk, a pharmaceutical company with a 30% weight in the index. The company showed amazing growth during the period, significantly contributing to the spectacular climb of the KAX.

In the FX, since the sudden weakening of the Euro began with the introduction of NIRP by the ECB in June 2014, an argument could be made for the policy's impact. In the rate of inflation, however, the impact might not be easily seen. Any pickup in inflation in the area was more likely once again due to the global economic recovery from early 2009 and QE by the ECB.

Last but not least, according to the common scenario shared by central banks, NIRP should have induced the flow of funds into housing loans, activating housing markets. This scenario apparently played out in the Swedish housing market. The notable difference between the housing markets in Japan and Sweden was that Sweden had accepted a large number of immigrants at the time, which contributed significantly to the revitalization of the housing market. In Japan, by and large a nation closed to immigrants, the impact was expected to be more limited.

The widely accepted view on the BoJ's motivation in introducing NIRP is that the BoJ hoped to generate change in the investment and consumption behavior of individuals and corporations alike. In fact, the fall in the long-term yields induced by NIRP not only resulted in the fall of housing and apartment loan interest rates but also in the cancellation of some yield-correlated MMFs.

The fall in the housing and apartment loan interest rates has generated a considerable increase in privately owned homes in some urban areas, but more notable has been the mushrooming of apartment complexes in rural areas, which the media has already called a "bubble." While the creation of unnecessary mass-housing units was perhaps an unintended consequence of NIRP, the policy's effect on the increase in capital spending or private investment is still in doubt.

When we look at the history of capital spending, we see that both its increase and decrease are closely correlated with the ups and downs of the TOPIX. The economic impact of capital spending only becomes known after some time has passed. This delay suggests, therefore, that the TOPIX is not likely responding to the fluctuation in capital spending. Accordingly, that a rise of the TOPIX prompts an increase in capital spending seems to make more sense than the other way around.

As discussed in the "OECD CLI" section in Chapter 1, the TOPIX is highly correlated with the G7 economy mid- to long-term. In other words, the TOPIX is a measuring stick of the global economy, and hence, there is no mystery in Japanese corporations' increasing or decreasing capital spending based on the TOPIX. In a way, interest rates are only secondary and perhaps not as important in making capital spending decisions.

What about the impact on consumer spending? The Japanese cabinet office publishes an index monthly called the consumer attitude index, which, very much like the consumer sentiment index in the US, is designed to measure consumer mindset. When viewed historically, this index also has high correlation with the TOPIX.

As of March 2015, the total financial assets held by Japanese households amounted to JPY1,700 trillion, of which JPY880 trillion was attributed to cash deposits and fixed income assets and JPY170 trillion to equities. From this statistic, at the time, we could see that a rising equity market would likely improve consumer sentiment. We could also see that if investment behavior changed among the general public and 5% of the JPY880 trillion got shifted to equities, the impact would supersede that of the GPIF, as some JPY44 trillion would flow into the equity market. As of August 2017, however, there was no evidence that NIRP had brought about such a change.

Impact of Consumption Tax Hikes

Tax hikes, whether the hike involves the consumption tax or other taxes, are said to be detrimental to the economy and therefore to the equity market. In Japan, however, the examples of consumption tax hikes are few and far between, such that it seems rather presumptuous to say that consumption tax hikes are bad for the equity market altogether.

An often talked-about example is the consumption tax hike (from 3% to 5%) that came into effect on April 1, 1997, under the watch of then PM Ryutaro Hashimoto. The Japanese equity market continued to rise after the hike until July of that year, only to capitulate soon after and turn in a poor performance until the end of 1998. But to blame the consumption tax hike of April 1997 for the abysmal equity market performance afterward is probably wrong, as the Asian financial crisis that broke out in July had a far more significant impact. Indeed, the movement of the Japanese equity market at the time more or less mimicked that of the S&P 500.

I do not mean to say that the consumption tax hike had zero impact on the Japanese equity market or economy. Rather, I mean that the impact of the aforementioned Asian financial crisis and the bankruptcy of the LTCM induced by the collapse of the Russian ruble was far more significant.

The first consumption tax hike took place in April 1987. Since Japan was in the midst of the bubble economy, perhaps the aftereffect of the tax hike at the time may not offer much to study. What about the consumption tax hike in April 2014? The Japanese equity market rose for a few days after the tax hike went live, falling afterward, but it began to rise again from mid-May.

Here, I will not repeat the description of the Japanese equity market in "Abenomics Market II." Suffice it to say that while the news value of the consumption tax hike was present, the Japanese equity market once again moved largely in line with the S&P 500, and the impact of the consumption tax hike itself was scarcely visible either on the Japanese economy or on the Japanese equity market.

The observations hitherto seem to say that historically, consumption tax hikes have only had a limited effect on the Japanese equity market as a whole. This may not be surprising, as the Japanese equity market responds more acutely to global economic conditions than to domestic demands. Looked at more closely, however, consumption tax hikes did have some visible impact on sector performance.

Comparing the TOPIX33 sector performances, after the 1989, 1997, and 2014 consumption tax hikes, sectors that showed particular strength were food, pharmaceutical, service, retail, and electrical appliances, all sensitive to consumer behavior. The reason why these sectors performed well could be that the tax hikes did not affect consumer behavior as much as initially feared.

The Fed

The central bank in the US is the Federal Reserve System (FRS) and with its governing body, the Federal Reserve Board (FRB), is known as the Fed. In America, investors are proverbially taught not to "fight with the Fed," which, its true meaning aside, speaks for the importance of central bank policies.

The role of the central bank, simply put, is to stabilize the economy, and to this end, tools such as policy rates (federal funds rates, or FFR; see Figure 2.2) and quantitative easing (or tightening) are employed. Policy rates, in this context, refer to the interest rates charged by the central bank on private banks, the common borrowers, and quantitative easing (QE) refers to the Fed's purchasing of treasury bonds, thereby supplying the market with liquidity and lowering long-term yields. Since the prices of treasury bonds are inversely proportional to their yields, the demand

FIGURE 2.2 FFR since 1990

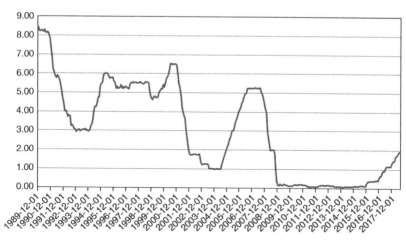

Source: FRED

from the central bank pushes down the interest rates to stimulate the economy.

When the economy heats up and the rate of inflation begins to rise, the central bank raises short-term rates to cool down the economy. Conversely, if deflation is about to threaten the health of the economy, the central bank lowers the short-term rates and, if that is not enough, guides the long-term rates lower to prop up the economy.

The Fed's policy impact is naturally tremendous on the US stock market, but it is also immeasurable on the Japanese stock market. How, then, can we utilize this impact in the construction of strategies appropriate for investing in Japanese equities? The textbook formulas suggest that since raising of interest rates by the central bank is intended to put a brake on the economy, it should work negatively on the equity market. On the other hand, lowering of interest rates is intended to speed up the economy and thus should work positively on the equity market.

In reality, the textbook formulas often don't work as expected. As will be discussed below in the "FX and the Japanese Equity Market" section, the Japanese equity market has experienced increased sensitivity to the FX rates since 2008. The reason is that the Fed was much more aggressive on monetary easing than the BoJ, which shrunk the interest rate spreads between the two nations, driving the Japanese yen higher as a result. One of the important factors that affect FX is the interest rate spread between two or more nations. If the US raises interest rates and Japan does nothing, the US interest rates will rise relative to those of Japan, which induces buying of the US dollar and selling of the Japanese yen, thereby lowering the relative value of the yen. As stated earlier, a weaker yen is generally positive for Japanese equities. Consequently, although the Fed is trying to cool down the economy by raising rates, Japanese equities tend to go higher. Regarding this phenomenon, however, the following clarification needs to be added.

The Fed raises rates because it believes that the economy is improving or already strong. As the economy gets stronger, yen carry trades become more active. "Yen carry trades" refers to borrowing the low-interest-rate Japanese yen, and selling it to exchange for higher-interest-rate foreign currencies, which contributes to a weaker JPY. On the other hand, an improving economy entails buying of equities. Particularly Japanese equities, sensitive to the ups and downs of the global economy, are often bought ahead of equities of other nations.

In other words, a weaker JPY and stronger equity market are happening simultaneously in this case, one not necessarily causing the other. On the surface, however, it looks as though the weaker JPY is causing the Japanese equity market to go up. As suggested earlier, investors also buy or sell Japanese equities because they expect the currency to move in certain directions.

If Fed rate hikes directly translated to a higher equity market, nothing could be simpler. The reality, as usual, is more complicated. I wrote before that strategists learn from history and pass judgment on the present and future, just as doctors learn from accounts of past illnesses. The difficulty of judging how Fed rate hikes affect the Japanese equity market is that there are only a handful of historical cases available and the patterns are by no means straightforward.

Table 2.2 lists the state of the US economy and EPS growth of the S&P 500 Index (index weighted average of the constituent stocks) for the five times preceding 2016 that the Fed decided to raise the federal fund rate (FFR) after a long hiatus. Real GDP Growth, Nominal GDP Growth, Durable Goods Growth, IP Growth, and SPX EPS Growth all refer to the year-on-year (YoY) change. Before these hikes, the Fed had been lowering or keeping FFR steady for some time.

TABLE 2.2 First Fed interest rate hikes and the US economy

	Real GDP Growth	Nom GDP Growth	Durable Goods Growth	IP Growth	SPX EPS Growth	ISMPMI
February 1994	2.60%	5.00%	6.80%	3.07%	16.84%	56.50%
March 1997	4.60%	6.40%	2.40%	7.30%	11.53%	53.80%
June 1999	4.60%	6.30%	5.50%	4.38%	5.66%	55.80%
June 2004	4.20%	7.10%	7.30%	2.25%	26.11%	60.50%
December 2015	2.40%	1.70%	1.70%	4.82%	4.00%	52.90%

Source: FRED

At first glance, though the year 2015 may not exactly fit the mold, the US economy was quite strong each time the Fed raised interest rates. The pattern after the first FFR hike is not uniform, however. After the February 1994 hike, the Fed raised rates six times until February 1995, but the 1997 rate hike was done only once in March. After the June 1999 hike, with a strong economy and the internet bubble as a backdrop, the Fed raised rates five times until May 2000. The June 2004 rate hike, on the other hand, was followed by sixteen more rate hikes over the next two years.

It goes without saying that the Fed rate hikes are conducted with an eye on the economy, just as investors make their investment decisions based on how they view the state of the economy. The difficulty of judging the impact of Fed rate hikes resides in this fact.

Based on the limited samples, the general trend is that the equity market tends to display strength going into the first rate hike. Since the Fed decides to raise rates basing its judgment on strong economic data, a strong equity market is perhaps no surprise. The flipside of the strong equity market before rate hikes is that, generally, the equity market weakens after rate hikes. Again, this is no surprise, as the Fed raises rates to slow down the economy.

As for the peculiarity of the Japanese equity market, perhaps its outstanding performance upon Fed rate hikes should be noted, as apparent in the performance of the MSCI indices. Among the various indices provided by the MSCI are the MSCI World Index (which covers developed markets) and the MSCI Emerging Markets Index. The past pattern shows that the MSCI Emerging Markets Index tended to outperform the

MSCI World Index when the Fed was raising rates. The exception was the MSCI Japan Index, which tended to outperform the MSCI Emerging Markets Index 50% of the time. This trend might be attributed to the currency factor, but whatever the case, upon Fed rate hikes, the Japanese equity market has behaved very much like emerging equity markets.

Broad generalizations should always be taken with a grain of salt, however. In 1999, due to "irrational exuberance," the equity market continued to rise despite the rate hikes, and in 2004, the succession of rate hikes failed to prevent the impressive performance of the Japanese equity market from mid-2005 to mid-2006. On the other hand, after the December 2015 rate hike, what we saw was a crumbling equity market in January 2016. As seen in Table 2.2, the less-than-robust US economy in December 2015 could have allowed us to predict the abysmal equity market performance in the following month.

The issue is whether there is a gap between the economic reality and what the Fed believes to be the economic reality. Of course, what we use to measure the economic reality also makes a difference. What if we use the OECD CLI as the measuring stick of economic reality and see what can happen if the Fed raises rates when this indicator is pointing down?

There were actually four such periods in the last 25 years. The first period was from August 1994 to June 1995; the second, from November 1999 to December 2000; the third, from June 2004 to April 2005; and the fourth, from December 2015 to January 2016. In the first case, the TOPIX plummeted 27%; the second, down 22%; the third, down 5%; and the fourth, down 7.5%. In all these cases, the market was struck by the double blows of a weakening economy and Fed rate hikes.

FX and the Japanese Equity Market

Day-to-day observers of the Japanese equity market know that the market returns are highly correlated with the movement of the currency. What we see is that the overall equity market tends to rise when the value of JPY falls, and vice versa. We may say that if we know which way the currency is headed, we will know which way the Japanese equity market is headed. If we know the direction of the currency, however, there is no point in investing in equities, as we should directly invest in the FX market via FX futures, rather than the equity market.

This said, since many institutional investors are tied to the equity market such that they can only invest in equities, understanding the movement of the FX market becomes doubly important. Of course, this is easier said than done. Predicting the direction of a given currency is often difficult even for FX specialists.

In addition, what makes the matter more complicated is that the equity-currency correlation depends on the period where the correlation is measured and even shows sudden changes at times. Relying on the views on FX when investing in Japanese equities, therefore, is generally ill-advised.

When we limit our observation to the US dollar–Japanese yen relationship, the rates, unsurprisingly, depend on the nations' monetary policies over the long run. As discussed in the "Abenomics" section above, monetary base growth has a notable impact on the dollar-yen rate. This is akin to saying that the rate of inflation has close ties to monetary base growth, a textbook phenomenon.

Needless to say, the correlation is by no means 100%, as usual. The JPY weakened significantly against the USD from 2005 to 2006, but the monetary base growth in the US was far larger than that of Japan. If the monetary base growth had been the only factor, then the JPY should have strengthened against the USD. Instead, the factor that moved the JPY in the opposite direction was the Fed rate hikes.

In 2004, the severely damaged world economy due to the collapse of the internet bubble began to show signs of recovery (though the OECD CLI was in the negative territory), and the Fed, fearing inflation, decided to raise the FFR in June. As the economy further strengthened, the pace of the rate hikes picked up, and by June 2006, the Fed ended up raising rates seventeen times, as stated before. Consequently, the FFR was hoisted from 1% to 5.25%, and the JPY weakened against the USD by about 20% in the process.

The Nikkei 225 saw its bottom in October 2004 and its peak in April 2006, gaining some 65% during this time—the so-called Koizumi Bull Market after then PM Junichiro Koizumi. As the name suggests, the spectacular performance of the Koizumi Bull Market should probably not be solely attributed to the weak JPY. Table 1.3 tells us that the G7 economy was already in its recovery phase by May 2005, and the equity market likely responded to this among other signs of an economic rebound.

In addition, Junichiro Koizumi was known for his restructuring agenda and was popular particularly among foreign investors, who, as a result, decided to invest heavily in the Japanese equity market.

As noted in the previous section, whether a strong equity market invites a weaker yen or the other way around is often a subject of debate. The answer probably lies midway between, meaning that either is possible depending on circumstances.

Investors are said to be "risk-on" when their risk tolerance increases. When investors are risk-on, money, by definition, flows from low-risk bonds to high-risk equities, and the JPY generally gets sold. By looking at the history of JPY weaknesses, we can identify a few reasons as to why the JPY is sold when investors are risk-on.

If we limit the history to after 1990, one dominant factor that drove JPY weaknesses was the yen carry trade by hedge funds and others. As touched upon earlier, this is the trade where investors borrow the low-interest Japanese yen and sell it for higher-interest-rate foreign currencies as an investment. Another JPY weakness factor was investment in higher-interest rate foreign currencies by Japanese households and retail investors. In either case, the trades are executed only when the FX environment is deemed more or less stable (i.e., risk taking is done at higher tolerance levels).

When the world economy teeters or the finance of some country goes sour, the tolerance level drops, so that investors become "risk-off" and the piled up "risk-on" trades are met with a drastic unwinding of positions. This is the mechanism that drives the JPY stronger at risk-off times.

An additional factor that contributes to JPY weakness in an equity bull market to a lesser extent is the selling of the JPY by foreign equity investors as an FX hedge. When the prices of Japanese equities rise and the portfolio market capitalization becomes larger, portfolio managers are faced with increased FX risk, which can be lessened by short selling the currency.

The US state pension fund I worked for, incidentally, did not hedge its FX exposure at all. In addition to the absence of currency traders and necessary middle- and back-office structures, the fact of the matter was that, historically, gains marked by the equity upside were much larger than the loss incurred by the currency downside, which reduced the need for a hedge. I suspect that many of the other US pension funds as well as hedge funds also do not hedge their FX exposure.

The mechanisms discussed up to this point are not the sole currency movers. Speculators that understand these processes use the opportunities to sell or buy the JPY. We also witnessed more than once a buying of USD or JPY as safe havens during the Euro crises.

We often hear, "Japan is no longer an export nation" and "a dominant part of the nation's GDP comes from domestic consumption." The equation where a cheap JPY leading to a higher equity market has not changed markedly since the mid-2000s, however, and as long as a majority of investors believe in this equation, it is unlikely to change.

Predicting the daily movement of a currency is just as hard as predicting that of the equity market. As will be discussed in Chapter 4, "Market Tops and Bottoms," there are a handful of day-traders who claim to have achieved considerable wealth by utilizing "charts" and other short-term methods in trading FX and equities. If their methods had been foolproof, however, they would have been the wealthiest individuals in the world by now. The fact of the matter is that they are not, which implies that there is a limitation to their methods.

Whatever the case may be, I possess neither the skills nor the knowledge that allows me to profit from short-term technical signals. Accordingly, what will be considered here is the kind of stocks that need to be bought if we can more or less predict the movement of FX mid- to long-term.

When investors expect the JPY to weaken, immediately they go for stocks of exporters or companies with a large overseas presence. A weak JPY means a competitive edge for Japanese products and increased profits when overseas earnings are converted without FX hedge to the Japanese currency. The existence of these companies contributes to Japan's being almost a perpetual current surplus nation, as the process of conversion from overseas currencies to Japan's own currency entails buying of the JPY.

Many of these companies, as a matter of fact, not only disclose their earnings sensitivity to FX but also the FX rate they use to forecast earnings. Thus, if the JPY goes lower (cheaper) than what these companies expect, earnings will likely go higher as a result. These FX-sensitive companies are typically of the automobile and auto-related sector, precision instruments sector, steel sector, and electrical appliances sector, but not exclusively. Since more than a handful of companies in the pharmaceutical, food, chemical, and other sectors also have overseas revenue exposure, each company needs to be examined carefully for its FX-sensitivity.

Moreover, there is a strong likelihood that if we buy just stocks of exporters and companies with large overseas business exposure, we may underperform the overall market when the FX moves to a weaker JPY. As stated earlier, a weak JPY is a "risk-on" phenomenon, and when the overall market is "risk-on," stocks of so-called cyclical companies tend to be preferred by investors.

Cyclical companies are not just exporters or those with overseas exposure. They can come from domestic-demand sectors such as real estate, banks, securities and trading, and insurance. Even railway stocks often see substantial upside when the economy is on the recovery. In particular, stocks of securities and trading companies tend to see the largest upside when the JPY moves to the weak side.

A quick way to figure out which stocks will likely go up in response to FX moves is to calculate the correlation coefficient between the change in USD-JPY rates and stock returns. As stated earlier, the correlation coefficient thus calculated depends on both the length of the measurement and frequency of the returns, but experience tells us that an ideal length of measurement is from one to two years and ideal returns are from three to five days.

Aside from these factors, we also note that risk-on markets are usually led by the futures, which cause the entire equity index to rise. If the Nikkei 225 futures are bought, the constituent stocks of the Nikkei 225 index will rise. In this case, stocks that are heavily weighted in the index should see the largest increase in funds flow. If we are talking about the present-day Nikkei 225, the heavily weighted stocks are stocks like Fast Retailing and Softbank, among others.

To sum up, "risk-on" implies a weaker JPY and stronger equity market, and "risk-off," the other way around. When "risk-on," investors should buy not only FX-sensitive stocks but also cyclical stocks and stocks with large weights in broader indices.

US Presidential Elections

The weight of the US economy among its global peers is large, and countless nations are listed as America's trading partners. Consequently, ups and downs in the US economy are literally those of the world economy. Because the equity market is a mirror of the economy as well as the human psyche, if the economy improves, so does the equity market, and vice versa. When the equity market rises above and beyond what the state of the economy justifies, the market may be called a "bubble."

The state of the economy is perhaps most easily fathomed by the nation's GDP. An expanding GDP directly translates to an expanding economy. GDP can be defined in several ways, but the difference is only in expression. Ultimately, the definitions are all the same and expressed as $GDP = Consumption + Investment + Government \ Spending + Net \ Export$.

The above equation tells us that GDP largely depends on the nation's monetary, fiscal, and trade policies. In the "Impact of Consumption Tax Hikes" section above, we saw no evidence that consumption tax hikes generated deterioration in the economy mid- to long-term, but viewed short-term, we cannot deny that consumer behavior is negatively affected. Investment and import-export are obviously affected by the nation's monetary and taxation policies, and government spending, by definition, fiscal policy.

Since just which way the nation's economy is headed largely depends on who becomes the leader, what she or he will propose as economic policies, and how those policies are executed, the post of the US presidency is of grave importance. How, then, do US presidential elections affect the equity market?

The answer presumably depends on who becomes the president and what kind of policies are being proposed. Does this mean that if we know who becomes the president and what the promised policy changes are, we will know which way the Japanese equity market is headed?

Of course not. We must also know how practical the promised policies are, and to know the practicality, we may need to know which party holds the majority seats in the House of Representatives or Senate, who the leaders of both houses are, whether those leaders or other influential politicians will agree with the president, and perhaps many other related issues. Even if the proposed policies are swiftly approved by both houses and signed by the president, we may want to know how much time is needed before the policies will have material impact on the economy.

These questions generally do not have easy answers. Trying to find out these answers might seem worthwhile, but when we consider the time and effort it may take to get to the answers, these factors may turn out to be nothing but "noise." While we are examining these issues and factors, the market may begin to move on different issues and factors. Worthwhile factors at present may become obsolete by the time investment decisions are made.

A good example for this is the Trans-Pacific Partnership (TPP). Although the details of the TPP may not be well known, from the news reports, at least its name should be familiar to most readers. "TPP" more accurately stands for the "Trans-Pacific Strategic Economic Partnership Agreement" and refers to a free-trade agreement among twelve Pacific-rim nations.

The TPP initially encountered strong objections domestically in Japan as well as abroad, but after several adjustments and negotiations, the Japanese cabinet office released its details on October 20, 2015. It was a ground-breaking agreement signed by the US, Canada, Australia, Japan, and others, intent on lowering or abolishing tariffs on agricultural and industrial products, as well as liberalizing the flow of financial products, and the market took immediate notice.

The prudence of considering the TPP as a factor in trading stocks at the time remains questionable to this day, however. Even though the agreement had been reached, it was limited to the agreement among emissaries. The emissaries needed to go back to their own countries and attain parliamentary or congressional approval. Additionally, to execute the agreement, it was expected to take years if not decades, rendering its economic impact opaque at best.

This said, the stock market is a casino, and as such, if many consider a fixed theme as the dominant factor, the stocks related to that factor are bound to move. In this sense, perhaps jumping on the TPP band-wagon might not have been completely meaningless and some investors might have generated a profit because of it. The logic behind the theme, however, was feeble, as stated above.

We cannot circumvent Donald Trump when discussing the TPP. Donald Trump had expressed his opposition to the TPP during his race for the US presidency, and when elected, immediately nullified the agreement. Investors that had bought TPP-related stocks, expecting a smooth ratification of the agreement, presumably faced a considerable loss on the choices they had made. In reality, TPP-related stocks soared like an eagle from the day Donald Trump was elected president.

The reason for the seemingly mysterious price appreciation was that most of the TPP-related stocks were also cyclical stocks. Needless to say, the TPP was not the only issue on his agenda when Mr. Trump ran for office. Among others, massive tax cuts and deregulation aimed at revamping the US economy, and investment in the US infrastructure, were also promised. Cyclical stocks' responding strongly to his victory was therefore no surprise. These stocks continued to rise until March 13, 2017, a temporary peak of the TOPIX. Among the top gainers were Dai-ichi Life and other insurance stocks, JFE, and other steel makers, all in line with Donald Trump's promised policies.

Recall that the TPP is just one example of broader presidential poli-cies. Generally speaking, we are not certain how well these policies will be executed or how long it will take for them to have meaning-ful economic impact. Even if the stock market rises on the hopes and expectations, the impact by itself is unlikely to last too long.

Donald Trump became the 45th president of the US, advocating rather drastic policy measures and changes on many fronts. Unlike him, most presidents tend to choose more or less middle-of-the-road policies, be it social or economic.

Whatever the case may be, the common thread among all past pres-idents is that they promised policies aimed at improving the nation's economy as they campaigned for office. As stated earlier, at the time of the election, whether the policies will be implemented and succeed is not easily assessed. Indeed, when viewed historically, the stock mar-ket reaction to presidential elections is not all that spectacular, unlike the case with the election of President Trump.

What if we viewed presidential elections' effects on the world's econ-omy longer term? Perhaps the OECD CLI can shed light on this effect. Figure 2.3 shows (the vertical straight lines mark the date of US presi-dential elections) that in most cases, the G7 OECD CLI tends to rise at the same time as or slightly after the date of US presidential elections. We have already seen the high correlation between the OECD CLI and the TOPIX, and hence we can argue that US presidential elections tend to have a positive impact on the Japanese equity market.

The impact may not be as impressive as the election of Donald Trump as the US president, but we can see the general positive impact of US presidential elections on the global economy, nevertheless.

A slight departure from the topic of US presidential elections takes us to the impact of political turmoil on the equity market. Since his election, Donald Trump has suffered a great deal in his public approval ratings and cabinet rebellions, not to mention the existence of scandalous disclosures, whether true or not.

Though President Trump, as of October 2017, continued to struggle with low approval ratings, the US stock market could not be more robust. The ISMPMI jumped above 60 in September, and the S&P 500 followed

FIGURE 2.3 US presidential election and G7 OECD CLI

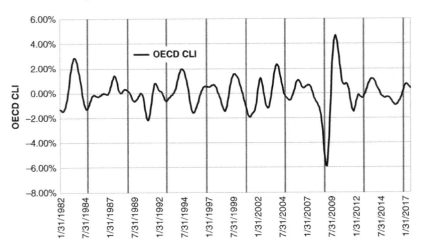

Source: OECD

suit. Even if the spectacular rise was due to the expected passage of the large tax-cut bill, the phenomenon only confirmed that ultimately the stock market is a mirror of the economy, and politics is secondary.

On the other hand, when Watergate was hot on American TV from 1973 to 1974 (Richard Nixon resigned in August 1974), the S&P 500 crumbled. At first glance, it looks as though the political scandal had negatively affected the stock market, but the truth was that inflation was sharply rising from early 1973 on, and the Fed had to aggressively raise rates in succession to stop it. Almost simultaneously, we saw a marked deterioration of the ISMPMI.

There is no doubt that the US stock market was responding to this. To make matters worse, OPEC forced oil embargo on the nations that supported Israel in the Yom Kippur War, which led to the so-called first oil crisis. The rate of inflation spiked and equity markets globally plummeted.

The impact of Watergate might have been hidden behind the global catastrophe, but nevertheless, what we saw was a stock market taking a blow from the economy and not the political scandal.

CHAPTER 3

Topics Derivatives

The word "derivatives" is no longer strange vocabulary even for someone unfamiliar with the financials industry. Derivatives include the totality of the financial tools connected to futures and options, and for outsiders, they conjure the image of something highly mathematical and hard to understand. Due to their complex façade, derivatives are often treated like monsters and blamed for market catastrophes.

The title of this chapter actually has a double meaning. The first meaning is an obvious one: the chapter literally talks about market impact due to derivative instruments, which not only include futures and options but also broader instruments such as ETFs and index-related strategies. The second meaning is that subjects covered here may not be mainstream topics; in other words, as general investors seek investment strategies in Japanese equities, these subjects may not seem as important as more traditional subjects.

If these subjects are not as important as more traditional ones, then the question is whether these subjects are "noise." The answer is that these are "noise" sometimes but not other times. Put differently, whether "noise" or not depends on how they are used. The essence of this statement hopefully will become clearer later on, but be that as it may, investors can make their own judgment if, and only if, they know the nature of these subjects.

Even if investors do not trade futures, options, or ETFs, knowing about them should give some theoretical comfort when trading common stocks. At least no one will laugh at knowledgeable investors for not knowing about these subjects. Not only that, but such investors will have acquired some bragging rights for knowing about them, because derivatives simply cannot be ignored when trying to wholly understand the ups and downs of the equity market.

Volatility

"Volatility" is not a strange word even for those unfamiliar with the equity market. Whether in equities, FX, or fixed income instruments, volatility refers to the amount or the rate of change in the price of the underlying financial instruments. In general, volatility is the annualized standard deviation of the daily returns (commonly denoted as σ).

The standard deviation measures how much the numbers deviate from their average, and when the numbers are normally distributed, one standard deviation denotes the probability of the numbers remaining between 1σ and -1σ to be about 68%.

Naturally, the standard deviation depends on the timeframe where the average is taken. Accordingly, volatility of a time series depends on the period of measurements. As a rule, when the short-term volatility is high, so is the long-term volatility, but this is just a general tendency. The price movement of financial instruments depends on the economy as well as the era; hence, low one-month volatility may not necessarily indicate low one-year volatility.

In the options market, volatility plays a key role. In the Black-Scholes model, used to price options, volatility is one of the needed variables. Prices of options are determined based on the projected price of the underlying instruments in the future, and obviously future prices depend on their volatility.

It is also obvious that the volatility used to calculate option prices is the projected future volatility. In industry jargon, the projected future volatility is called implied volatility, and is distinguished from historical volatility, which is uniquely calculated from past data. Incidentally, since no one is certain of the future price movement, implied volatility, in most cases, is deduced from some mathematically-adjusted form of historical volatility.

Let us assume that, in the past, one-month volatility of the Nikkei 225 was 10%. What does this number mean? Using 20 trading days as one month, the rate of daily change is calculated to be about 0.6%. If the Nikkei 225 was JPY20,000, then if the index oscillated by JPY120 per day, the volatility would be about 10%, and if the index oscillated by 1% (JPY200), then the one-month volatility would rise to 16.3%.

The average one-month volatility of the Nikkei 225, calculated from 1990, is 22.2%, and since 2009, after the global financial crisis, the average one-month volatility is 21.5%. The former number suggests that the Nikkei 225 moved about 1.1% per day, which, when calculated using 20,000 as the base value, leads to JPY220 per day.

For many observers of the Nikkei index, the number may appear puzzling, as the experience tells them that they do not often see the index move by JPY220 per day. The puzzlement stems from the base value, because the Nikkei 225 near JPY20,000 is not realistic. Since 1990, the Nikkei 225 has seldom been above JPY20,000, and accordingly, the 1.1% daily move only meant JPY88 or JPY110.

We also note that the 1.1% daily move is on the average. For example, if the Nikkei 225 moves by 3% per day during just four days out of twenty, and moves 0% for sixteen days, the one-month volatility rises to above 20%. The impression from the experience—the Nikkei 225 did not move JPY220 per day—therefore seems correct.

Volatility also has some interesting features that general investors should be aware of even if they do not trade options. One: volatility tends to mean-revert. This feature is probably intuitive. When something changes, the rate of change is not constantly large but generally goes up and down. Equity prices, in particular, unless the underlying companies go bust, tend to fluctuate around certain levels.

Two: volatility tends to rise when the underlying prices fall, and vice versa. A simple reason for this phenomenon is that a drop in the equity price or index generally results from a surprise, while a rise comes as more or less expected. As discussed in the "ISMPMI" section in Chapter 1, this is a reflection of the human psyche and only goes to prove that the equity market is a mirror of human minds.

Remember, when we hear of good news, we seldom act immediately. We are skeptical at first, and only after being reasonably convinced do we act. In other words, humans are suspicious and careful by nature. When we hear of bad news, on the other hand, we tend to act immediately to avoid the risk. Only after we act do we look into the facts, and if the facts are straight, we take comfort; if not, we try to undo the initial action.

When the equity market goes up on good news, the stocks are being bought "carefully," and thus, the volatility on the upside is more under control. When the equity market goes down on bad news, investors rush to dump stocks to lessen the risk, and thus the volatility on the downside becomes more pronounced.

Needless to say, the above prescription is not 100% foolproof. Indeed, there have been some exceptional cases where the market volatility rose on the upside. One case that comes to mind is from November 2012 to January 2013, when the equity market jumped at the introduction of Abenomics. Another case is the period immediately following the surprising US presidential victory of Donald Trump.

Historical and Implied

As stated in the previous section, volatility can be thought of as either historical or implied. Since historical volatility is calculated from past time series data, it is also known as realized volatility. We also saw that implied volatility is a projected volatility whose calculation, to some extent, is based on volatility in the past.

When we plot implied volatility and historical volatility side by side, we see that implied volatility, in general, rises after and falls before historical volatility. There is a simple reason for this: options traders usually do not foresee a large movement in the stock market before it actually takes place, and thus they customarily react after the fact. Of course, if there is going to be a historical event, such as a US presidential election, then the market is expected to show more than usual movements, and therefore we often observe that implied volatility rises before the fact. A sudden and marked jump in implied volatility, known as a volatility spike, however, generally occurs only after a jump in historical volatility.

Once volatility jumps but is expected to come down in the future, then the implied falls before the historical. This is easily understood from the calculation of volatility, also described in the previous section.

In calculating one-month volatility, for example, the time series data from the last thirty days is used (assuming 1 month = 30 days). Strictly speaking, since the market is closed on Saturdays and Sundays, the time series data from the last twenty days is used, but the distinction here is beside the point.

If the last thirty-day time series data is being used, then only the incidents that took place during the thirty-day period contribute to the calculation. If the market had crashed thirty days earlier, and the realized volatility spiked as a result, then the volatility engendered by the initial market crash is destined to vanish thirty days after (since only thirty days' worth of data contributes to the volatility calculation). Option traders see this decline ahead of the time, and hence implied volatility declines ahead of historical volatility.

Here, I hasten to add that historical volatility is not the sole driver of implied volatility. There exist volatility funds as well as those that trade volatility as an asset. If volatility is traded as an asset, supply-demand imbalance enters into the equation, and implied volatility is affected by it.

It is not difficult to imagine that forecasting "near future" is easier than "far future." Accordingly, forecasting near-term volatility is easier than far-term volatility. Thus, while near-term implied volatility is more in line with near-term historical, far-term implied is more swayed by other elements.

Near-term implied volatility is by no means immune from supply-demand issues but less affected by them, as short-dated options enjoy greater liquidity. Long-dated options, on the other hand, often suffer low liquidity and, hence are more impacted by the demand of certain market participants.

In the following sections, we will view how transactions involving derivatives—mainly futures and options—affect the equity market, and how option-imbedded structures products affect volatility itself.

Futures Influence

The term "present value" should be familiar to anyone in the financial field. Goods or money have "present" and "future" values connected by the interest rate (if equities, add dividends). If the interest rate is positive, the present value will increase with time by the interest paid in the future, so the future value will necessarily be higher. This "future value" is the theoretical price of the futures (in Nikkei 225 or TOPIX futures, the present value will rise relative to the future value by the amount of the dividend paid).

Investors who trade futures can largely be divided into three categories. One group consists of speculators. If speculators believe that a bull market is ahead, they buy (index) futures, and if not, sell (index) futures. In theory, there should not be any arbitrage opportunities between futures and cash (otherwise risk-free profit would be possible), and thus buying of futures results in higher index value and vice versa, bestowing speculators power to move the market. As discussed in the "BoJ and Kuroda Bazooka" section in Chapter 2, when the market is overheated, often we see cash due to arbitrage trades mount to very high levels. As was the case on May 22, 2013, this is a warning sign.

Another group that actively trades futures are the hedgers. Many domestic institutional investors such as pension funds are among those in this group. They typically manage a considerable size of index funds, and hence if they wish to remain market neutral, they sell index futures against their portfolios. If they sell futures, the cash market will be exposed to downside pressure by the no-arbitrage principle. Thus, it looks as though the move is ill-advised. At least in theory, however, the hedge is structured to assure market neutrality, so the concern may be unjustified.

The third group of investors is the arbitragers, and their impact on the cash market is also limited. The future value and present value are related by the simple equation, as explained above, but sometimes the relationship becomes distorted by the demands from speculators and hedgers. Arbitragers try to take advantage of these opportunities.

If arbitragers believe that the futures market price is above the fair theoretical value, they sell futures and buy cash. If the opposite is the case, they sell cash and buy futures to take the spread. In Japan, index futures are settled quarterly on SQ. At that time, the futures price should match the cash price. In other words, the theoretical price matches the market price. Thus, had the futures been sold (bought) when the market price was expensive (cheap), a profit can be generated.

Viewed from the cash market, since futures and cash are traded in opposite directions (buy and sell, or vice versa), the impact of arbitrage activity is limited. Arbitragers have a pronounced impact, instead, on individual stocks. This, in fact, is similar to the impact due to index funds alluded to earlier.

Arbitrage opportunities between futures and cash generally arise based on the market sentiment (bullish or bearish), and interest rate and dividend expectations. To take advantage of arbitrage opportunities, arbitragers must hold a cash equity portfolio that exactly matches the index (whose futures they trade) in names and weights.

As a result, if there is going to be a change in index members, arbitragers need to buy and sell individual stocks based on the expected change. This is where the impact on individual stocks comes from. Since the process is very much similar to index funds, we will look into the details in the next section.

Impact of Index Funds

Index funds manage money by investing in indices, their performance measured either relative to the given indices or by the performance of the indices themselves. Those that measure relative performance are called active funds, and those that offer the performance of the indices themselves are called passive funds.

More narrowly, some call only passive funds "index funds," but here, in contrast to most hedge funds that offer absolute returns, we call all funds that offer index returns or returns relative to certain indices "index funds." The state pension funds that I worked with were index funds, both active and passive. Depending upon country allocations, indices relative to which the investment performance was measured naturally varied. For Japan, as is the case for most US pension funds, the index used was the MSCI Japan Index. For most domestic pension funds in Japan, the index of choice is the TOPIX, though there are some that use the JPX400, Nikkei 225, or others.

The basic approach taken by index funds is to align their portfolio performance to given indices. The measure of alignment is called the tracking error, which is an annualized spread of return between the portfolio and index.

For active funds, their mission is to outperform the given index, but the outperformance generally needs to be kept within a certain range. The reason is that large outperformance necessarily entails large volatility relative to the index, and thus, from the risk-management point of view, is considered undesirable.

The tracking error, therefore, is important even for active funds, and the returns are expected to remain within the predetermined tracking error. For passive funds, as their desirable performance is the index return, the tracking error needs to be minimized.

If we wish to keep our portfolio in line with a given index, a failsafe way is to purchase all the constituents' stocks in the index according to their weights. Indeed, managers of the passive Nikkei 225 Index fund generally hold all 225 stocks in their portfolios to achieve a 0% tracking error.

For the passive funds that track the MSCI Japan Index, since there are only about 300 stocks in the index, a similar approach may be taken. For the TOPIX, however, since there are more than 1800 stocks in the index and many of the stocks with smaller weights often suffer from limited liquidity, a general approach is just to hold stocks with higher liquidity and adjust their weights in the portfolio to minimize the tracking error.

For the management of active funds, whether the funds track the Nikkei 225 or MSCI Japan, the portfolio managers naturally need not hold all the index constituent stocks. A general approach is to hold a limited number of stocks in the portfolio to keep the tracking error within range and adjust the weights to achieve outperformance over the index. Needless to say, the ability of the portfolio managers is tested in this instance.

What about the impact of index funds on the overall equity market? Notwithstanding the unrealistic case of all equities being held by index funds, the most significant impact is felt by individual stocks.

Let us assume that a large index fund has just been created and that the fund is required to track the Nikkei 225. The fund needs to buy the Nikkei 225 constituents according to their weights in the index, and thus, from a view point of funds flow, the largest beneficiary is the stock with the largest weight in the Nikkei 225 Index, which, as this book was written, is Fast Retailing. The price of the Fast Retailing stock is likely to rise as a result, regardless of the company's business performance. Such is the impact of index-tracking funds: they can dominate stock price performance in spite of stock fundamentals.

The impact of the GPIF asset allocation change, discussed in Chapter 2, "Policy Impact," is a typical example of a massive index fund's having tremendous impact on individual stocks. Creation of funds by major insurers or asset managers is publicly available information, and thus, by following the disclosure, we should be able to take a guess at which stocks may be affected and to what degree as a consequence.

The impact of index funds, however, is not limited to those examples. In fact, more measurable impact may be observed at index rebalance. Index rebalance refers to a review and possible alteration of index constituent stocks. The criteria and frequency of the review vary depending on the host of the index, but the aim of this book is not to list the myriad of indices or index rules. Each index has its own rebalance rules and policies, and they are in the public domain.

Those versed in the rules of index reviews can guesstimate which stocks are to be added to or deleted from a given index. The stocks to be deleted will likely suffer from a selloff by index funds and the stocks added will likely gain from a buying activity. If investors can forecast the deletion and addition candidates ahead of a rebalance, then they should be able to make a profit by shorting the deletion and buying the addition candidates. The investment strategy that employs this method is commonly known as the suckerfish investment, and its history goes back quite a way.

Of course, if we could make a profit just by following index rebalance rules, nothing could be simpler. As usual, however, the reality is far more complicated than meets the eye.

First, there is the difficulty of timing. For major indices such as the Nikkei 225, MSCI Japan, and TOPIX, a few months before the actual rebalance date, large brokerage firms have already published index rebalance forecast reports. These reports, closely following the index rebalance rules, forecast stocks to be deleted and added, and estimate the demand from passive funds, translated into the daily transaction volume of each stock. Since the passive demand comes from the world's pension funds and insurers, as well as mutual funds and ETFs, there are naturally some divergences in their forecasts, but most commonly the passive demand is estimated to be less than 10% of the total market capitalization of the index.

Actual reports contain not only the names of deletions and additions, but also the stocks that will likely be most affected by the rebalance. Since every stock in a given index comes with an assigned weight, any alteration among constituent members generates a weight shift, possibly resulting in trades by index funds. The reports, therefore, customarily list affected stocks in the order of impact.

A difficulty in rebalance trades comes first from the suckerfish investors, who establish their positions (by going long on those positively affected and short on those negatively affected) when these reports are initially released. It is also likely that proprietary desks of major securities firms and event funds, which may have their own forecasting methods, have set up similar positions as well.

What these investors want, obviously, is to make a profit, so they do not have to wait until the actual index rebalance takes effect. Rather, it is probable that they close their positions before the event, thereby engendering a large volume of buy-and-sell orders. Upon release of index rebalance reports, we often bear witness to a selloff of deletion candidates and buying of addition candidates. For event funds and proprietary traders, these may provide a perfect occasion for unwinding their positions.

Transactions by passive funds generally take place right at the rebalance. This is because passive funds abhor tracking errors, as discussed earlier, and trading days before or after rebalance increases tracking errors. We may think then that we should just pay attention to the passive fund demand and buy or sell stocks accordingly. Actually, this strategy does not work all that well either.

Each stock has its own liquidity, and if someone puts a large bid in for illiquid stocks, the stock prices will likely respond by leaping to higher levels. The result is an increase in tracking error, which passive funds wish to avoid in the first place.

Passive funds commonly employ execution traders, whose primary mission is to ensure smooth trading while minimizing tracking error. Upon rebalance, how they trade deletion and addition names is largely up to the discretion of execution traders, which makes the price movement of these stocks less transparent.

Another source of difficulty in taking advantage of rebalance is the rules of index rebalance themselves. Each index has its own rules, as mentioned before, but the rules are often not clearly defined or even practical.

For the Nikkei 225, for example, a portion of the rules is left up to interpretation by the *Nikkei*. Likewise, for the MSCI Japan, the MSCI retains its discretion regarding its index rules, and the same is true for the TOPIX, the Tokyo Stock Exchange (TSE). Thus, while strictly going by the rules may allow us to know 90% of the deletion and addition candidates before an actual rebalance, often 10% are missed almost inevitably.

If the member selection rules are rigid, guesstimating deletion and addition candidates becomes a cinch, giving advantage to certain investors. So, index providers intentionally make the rules less transparent. Perhaps more cynically viewed, index providers themselves are not certain about their selection methodology and by inserting "up to our discretion" somewhere in their index rules, they protect themselves from unwanted criticism or even lawsuits.

This second reason is perhaps most apparent in the free-float-ratio adjustment. The free-float-ratio refers to the ratio of short-term equity holders to the total equity holders and is important in index reviews because these adjustments are used to determine equity weights in indices such as the MSCI Japan and TOPIX.

Deciding who the short-term or long-term equity holders are is not as easy as it sounds, however. If the holder is the original owner of the company or major banks (known as policy stakeholders), then the distinction may be easy, but whether those listed as major shareholders in the company reports are short-term or long-term investors is often not clear. Consequently, who are and who are not free-float investors is determined somewhat whimsically by the index providers, creating much ambiguity in the allocation of equity weights.

We have seen hitherto how index funds and suckerfish investors impact individual stocks, but to benefit from their actions, there are several important hurdles that need to be cleared. Indeed, as far as I know, there is only a handful of very able proprietary and day traders who are successful in taking advantage of the opportunities generated by index rebalance.

Influence of Structured Products

Structured products, to be discussed here, refer to option-imbedded fixed income instruments, which are commonly created for and sold to retail investors. In Japan, put-imbedded instruments are the mainstream, and the options are generally written on equity indices, single stocks, and the currency.

The equity index is mostly the Nikkei 225 and single stocks are mostly large-cap stocks. The structure of the put option is such that the strike is set at 100% of the initial underlying asset price, the knock-out barrier at 105%–110% of the strike, and the knock-in barrier is placed somewhere between 40% and 70% of the strike.

For those unfamiliar with option terminology, the "strike" refers to the price of the underlying asset at and beyond which the option can be exercised, the "knock-out barrier" is the price where the option becomes worthless, and the "knock-in barrier" is the price level beyond which the option becomes exercisable at the strike price. In the case of structured products, the knock-out barrier is described in the early redemption clause. The difference between the strike and knock-in barrier is that the strike is proportional to the value of the option, while the knock-in barrier is a simple level where the option becomes alive.

Ignoring the option premium for the sake of simplicity, if the strike was set at 100% of the initial asset price and the asset price drops to 80% at expiry of the option, then the value of the put option at expiry will be 20%. If, in addition, the knock-in barrier was set at 70% simultaneously, the asset price did not reach the barrier, and hence, the option expires worthless. If, on the other hand, the asset price fell to 60% at expiry, the knock-in barrier was breached, and the value of the put option is 40%.

As seen in these examples, the structure of the option itself is not all that complicated. Nevertheless, structured products can cause havoc in the price movement of the underlying asset. The reason is as follows.

Trading options is a contract between buyers and sellers. In the case of put-embedded structured products, retail investors buy the instruments in order to attain the income generated from them, which is equivalent to selling the embedded puts (i.e., investors sell puts and receive the premium as income).

The buyers of the put options are the securities firms that originated the structured products. In professional jargon, the retail investors are short-put and securities firms are long-put. Since retail investors buy structured products for their income, and since the knock-in barriers are set well below the strike, either they hold on to their instruments or wait until knock-out to repurchase similar products.

For securities firms that are on the opposite end, long-put positions are considered as risk. The reason is that the value of the put options depends on volatility, time to expiry, price of the underlying asset, and so on, so long-put holders are exposed to daily mark-to-market price fluctuations.

The risks obviously need to be hedged. While the risks associated with time and volatility are generally hedged by constructing opposite positions using listed options or over-the-counter options (the latter may not be a perfect hedge, however), the risk associated with the price movement of the underlying asset (called the delta [δ] risk) is hedged by trading the underlying asset (for single stocks) or futures of the underlying asset (for currencies and indices). This δ-hedge activity generates considerable impact on the price of the underlying asset on occasion.

It gets a little complex from here, but to understand the impact of the structured products, we cannot avoid a further complexity. As stated earlier, the value of options depends on elements such as the price and volatility of the underlying asset, time to expiry, and so forth. This means that the value of options possesses certain sensitivity to these elements.

These sensitivities are commonly called Greeks and literally denoted by Greek letters. One of these is the δ, which is the sensitivity to the price of the underlying asset. The δ is generally expressed by how much the option price moves per 1% move in the price of the underlying asset. If, therefore, the underlying asset price moves up by 1% and at the same time the price of the option moves up by 1%, then the δ is 100% or 1.

This number actually is the hedge ratio when the δ risk needs to be hedged. If the option price goes up by 1% when the underlying asset price goes up by 1%, then to hedge the risk (so that the position remains unaffected), the same amount of the underlying asset as the option needs to be sold. If the option price falls by 1%, on the other hand, the opposite needs to be done. Selling or buying an underlying asset according to the δ is called the δ hedge.

More concretely, if we are put-long on an index, we need to go long on the index futures by the amount specified by the δ. Note that the δ changes according to the change in the underlying asset price. This is because the value of an option is dependent on how far the underlying asset price is from the strike of the option.

Just to fill in a few basics about options, basics that can be found anywhere in textbooks, when the underlying asset price is at the strike of the option, the option is said to be at-the-money (ATM), when it is beyond the strike (upside on calls and downside on puts), the option is said to be in-the-money (ITM), and when it has not reached the strike, out-of-the-money (OTM).

The value of the put option increases when the underlying asset price falls, and hence, we must increase the hedge ratio in that case and decrease it when the asset price rises. In other words, when the underlying asset price falls, more futures need to be bought, and when the underlying asset price rises, the amount of futures needs to be reduced (the futures need to be sold).

Note that buying index futures when the index falls and selling index futures when the index rises amount to reducing index volatility. This is the same with long-call positions; in this instance, when the index rises, futures need to be sold (since for long-calls, futures are shorted for the hedge), and when the index falls, futures need to be bought, thereby once again lessening index volatility. Once this mechanism is understood, it becomes evident that hedging the short-put or short-call position will result in increasing volatility.

Let us now think of the situation where the underlying asset price of the structured product falls to a near knock-in barrier level. As we have already seen, as the underlying asset price falls, the securities firm, which is put-long, needs to buy more underlying asset for the hedge.

Recall that the knock-in barrier is the boundary where the option value either becomes zero or becomes the difference between the strike and the underlying asset price. Put another way, near the knock-in barrier, the change in δ (called γ) becomes the largest, and as soon as the knock-in barrier is breached, the underlying asset that has been bought up to that time suddenly needs to be sold.

Of course, in reality, as the underlying asset price approaches the knock-in barrier, an unlimited amount of underlying asset is not being bought, according to the theoretical δ. If the δ is expected to converge to -1, then appropriate adjustments have already been made before the knock-in barrier is breached. Even so, we should nevertheless see substantial selling of the underlying asset (or futures) close to the barrier, and indeed what appears to be the impact of this selling has been observed.

This said, occurrences of these observations are few and far between since the underlying asset price needs to fall 30% to 40% or even more before the knock-in barriers come into place. Probably the most notable occurrences took place in the autumn-to-winter period of 2008. This is the period of the global financial crisis, and not only the Nikkei 225 but also single stocks were severely impacted.

While no precise measurements are available, and we can only speak from the observed phenomenon, Nomura Holdings and Daiwa Securities Group, both of which are the giants of the brokerage industry in Japan, may present outstanding examples. Historically, of the two, Nomura boasts a larger market capitalization and generally lower stock price volatility. In pre-2008 market crashes, almost without exception, the magnitude of the stock price correction was much larger for Daiwa than for Nomura.

During the 2007–2008 global financial crisis, however, the situation flipped. The time series data shows that the magnitude of the price correction in Nomura shares went far beyond that of Daiwa Securities. Perhaps more than a single culprit could be spotted, but one culprit was likely the existence of the structured products. Indeed, in 2008, the number of structured products issued on Nomura Holdings was multifold that of Daiwa Securities.

As the mechanism of hedging dictates, securities firms that took on the Nomura Holdings structured products were put-long and had to δ hedge their positions by going long on Nomura Holdings shares. When Nomura shares were sold heavily in the market, with the share price coming close to the knock-in barrier, the firms were forced to sell Nomura shares in significant quantity, which probably contributed to the precipitous fall in the share price.

It is not difficult to imagine that a similar situation was taking place for the Nikkei 225 as well; certainly the precipitous fall in the Nikkei 225 may have triggered the knock-in puts of the structured products, causing a wholesale selloff of the Nikkei futures by securities firms. We cannot pinpoint the actual impact, unfortunately, as the selloff also undoubtedly came from institutional investors and macro funds trying to hedge their exposure.

That said, when the market is in freefall, what concerns portfolio managers is which stocks will likely be most impacted by the knock-in structure, if any. Fortunately, structured-product information is open to the public, and to guesstimate the whereabouts of the knock-in barriers is not a hard task. Since structured products are aimed at retail investors, the target stocks are generally large-cap and well-known names, and since the put structure needs to generate attractive income, the target stocks are also more volatile stocks.

So far, we have seen the potential malaise regarding the underlying asset prices caused by the knock-in barriers of structured products. Here, a question may arise as to the potential impact of the knock-out barriers since the knock-out barriers render options worthless. The quick answer to the question is that the impact is generally small. To understand this, we literally need to further understand the structure of the structured products.

A crucial point is that the barriers of structured products become effective only when the breach of the barriers is monitored and observed. The fact of the matter is that knock-in barriers are monitored continuously while the monitoring of knock-out barriers is done only every quarter. This difference in the monitoring process separates the significance of the two barriers.

If the monitoring is done continuously, the change in δ immediately reflects on the underlying asset, which may affect its price, as discussed above. On the other hand, if the monitoring is done every quarter, as is the case for knock-out barriers, by the time the monitoring date arrives, the change in δ may very well be discounted (i.e., the δ may already be zero).

Of course, if the knock-out barrier is breached on the day of the monitoring, the δ suddenly becomes zero, leading to a selloff of the underlying asset that has been bought for a hedge. This is a rather rare phenomenon, as we may imagine, and even if it happens, long option holders have likely reduced their positions before the fact, expecting the breach of the barrier, and hence, the impact probably won't be large.

Impact of Convertible Bonds

Convertible bonds (CBs) refer to the bonds accompanied by the right to equity conversion. As the aim of this book is not to make distinctions among convertible bonds, warrant bonds, convertible preferred shares, or sundry other forms of convertible instruments, the discussion here can be understood to apply to these various forms of fixed-income instruments with a conversion feature. As they stand, the impact these derivative instruments have on the underlying assets is similar, as it derives mainly from the δ hedge mechanism.

As the name implies, CBs are a type of bond issued by corporations to collect funds from investors. Generally, when corporations wish to entice investment money, they issue shares, bonds, or CBs.

If corporations issue shares, their shareholders' equity will increase, but their EPS (earnings per share) will decline, potentially negatively affecting the share price performance. If corporations issue bonds, the number of shares will not increase but debt will. Increased debt means increased leverage, which is not necessarily negative, but larger debt can strangle corporate finance, if the economy worsens or interest rates rise. The corporations may suffer a lower credit rating due to a higher debt-to-equity ratio, which also implies more difficulty in organizing new loans.

In the world of corporate finance, CBs figuratively sit between shares and bonds. As they are bonds, the issuance initially and technically does not decrease EPS, even though they generally count as shareholder equity. As stated earlier, however, convertible bonds come in different shapes and forms, and some have forms such that the right of conversion and the bond itself are treated separately for accounting purposes.

While the issuance initially and technically does not decrease EPS, in reality, as soon as the issuance of CBs is announced, the share price gets hammered with few exceptions. The drop in the share price comes from the potential dilution (upon future conversion) of existing shares (called a dilution ratio), and the percentage drop is largely in line with the percentage dilution.

In recent years, since the structure of CBs has increasingly become complex, to decipher the exact impact of dilution, we need to be versed in the prospectus of the issue. For example, a CB called a recap CB is designed so that the convertible is issued simultaneously with share buybacks. In this case, we often see the share price rise upon convertible issuance.

Additionally, for any issuance, if we are able to understand the market sentiment and corporate prospects to some extent, the issuance of CBs may sometimes provide us with an opportunity to buy the shares. Again, this is a generalization, but the share price that drops due to convertible issuance tends to get back on the recovery track by the second or third day after the drop, with the share price often reaching the pre-drop level within a week.

Let us now turn to the impact of the convertible bond δ hedge. Here again, we cannot ignore the existence of the hedge fund. Convertible bonds are issued by corporations primarily targeting retail investors, but a portion goes to global CB investors and a portion goes to hedge funds commonly known as convertible arbitrage funds.

The δ hedge impact comes from these convertible arbitrage funds. By now, it must be clear that the right of conversion is identical to a call option. The right of conversion comes with a fixed time by which the conversion is allowed (maturity), a conversion price (strike), and its value depends on the volatility of the underlying stock. Convertible arbitrage funds hold the option part of the CBs, and through δ hedge, makes a profit.

Since convertible arbitrage funds are call option long, the hedge should be equity short. If the share price rises, the short position needs to be added (by selling more shares), and if the share price falls, the short position needs to be lessened (by buying back shares). If the share price remains in a narrow range and moves up and down, since the funds are selling shares when the price is up and buying back when the price is down, they naturally end up making a profit.

This simple enough strategy may sound effective without holding option long positions. In theory, it is possible to sell shares outright when the share price goes up and buy them back when the share price goes down. If we repeat this process by using ample funds, we may be able to make a profit as well, but by the same token, we may also see a substantial loss in the process if, for some reason, the share price runs away in either direction.

By holding options long, we can prevent this "runaway" scenario. This prevention mechanism is related to a characteristic of the call option.

Recall that by exercising the call option, an investor will receive the underlying asset at strike (conversion) price. For general investors, that is the end of the game. For those that wish to hedge their option holding, as is the case for convertible arbitrage funds, the hedge is done by considering the option's δ, as discussed in the previous section.

For a long call position, the δ of the option increases as the underlying asset price rises relative to strike, and when the underlying asset price goes well beyond strike, the δ converges to 1, corresponding to the probability of exercise reaching 100%. When the underlying asset price falls relative to strike, the δ decreases and eventually becomes 0, meaning the probability of exercise has reached 0%.

If the hedge is done based on the δ, when the share price runs away on the upside, there will be a loss from the short equity position, but since the call option is held long, the loss will largely be cancelled out by the gain on the option's position. When the share price plummets, on the other hand, the equity long position does not exist due to the automatic reduction in the δ, so the loss will be limited to the option premium paid.

Incidentally, the largest rate of change in δ generally takes place around the strike, and hence by holding the option, the hedgers not only know how many shares they need to buy or sell but also what share price level will give them the chance to make the maximum profit.

We should also note that positions on single-stock options do not just come from CBs. Convertible arbitrage funds have call options from CBs, but the same stock may have outstanding options positions created and hedged by brokers. If the strikes of these single-stock options coincide with those of the options from the CBs, the hedge effect may become even more pronounced.

So far, we have covered the basic information needed to understand the impact of the δ hedge on the underlying equity. When the stocks go up, sell them, and when they go down, buy them back; this process is the process of the δ hedge for option long (γ long in the professional lexicon) positions, and its effect is called the γ effect.

One of the obvious features of the γ effect is to pin down the share price at a certain level (called the pin-risk), and the "certain level" tends to be around strike (conversion price). The γ also has the characteristic of becoming larger as the option's maturity approaches. As a result, we often see the share price pinned near the conversion price upon maturity of the

CB. Our aim in this section is to focus on the δ hedge as a contributing factor to this phenomenon.

This said, the share price being pinned down at the conversion price is not solely due to the γ effect. As noted earlier, if and when CB conversion takes place, a corresponding number of new shares will be issued to the CB holders. Thus, the expected increase in the number of existing shares adds downward pressure on the share price near the conversion price.

Many a time, we have seen the share price jump at maturity of the CB. The phenomenon, in fact, is not limited to maturity, but also witnessed at early redemption. The early redemption clause is often predicated on the share price's remaining above a certain level for a prolonged number of days. The effect of the early redemption clause, therefore, is to keep the share price below such a level.

The above analyses suggest that if we know the conversion conditions of a CB and purchase the underlying shares beforehand, we may benefit from the lifting of the pin-risk and conversion risk at maturity. Not all shares jump upon conversion or expiry of the CB, of course. With appropriate conditions met, however, we should at least keep in mind that statistics are in our favor.

The number of new shares issued upon conversion of a CB can be calculated by the following equation:

New shares issued = Size of the CB (in JPY)/Conversion price (in JPY)

If the δ is 50%, about 50% of the new shares issued are being used for the δ hedge. This estimation, however, is based on the assumption that all of the CBs issued are held by convertible arbitrage funds. In reality, it is safe to assume that a substantial portion of the CB issues are held by retail investors and CB funds.

The question is how to calculate the δ. The exact calculation of the δ is based on the option model and therefore cannot be readily discussed in this literature. If we could access a software that allows us to fathom theoretical option prices, however, the calculation is not all that complicated. As a ballpark measure, the option δ is about 50% at ATM (at-the-money).

Since the δ changes according to the underlying asset price levels (in the present case, the share price levels), by calculating the rate of change, the number of shares used for the δ hedge can be estimated.

If the number of shares approaches or even exceeds the average daily trading volume of the shares, we can expect significant impact.

To know which stocks are affected by the δ hedge or conversion price can also be guesstimated by observing the share price movement. If the share price appears to be repelled by or pinned to the conversion price, then changes in the share price as it reacts to the expiry or conversion of the CB are large.

The last subject of this section is the δ hedge or the γ effect, when options are held short. When the end-investors are long option, brokers often face this situation, as discussed earlier, but also, when the CB is equipped with multiple conversion prices, convertible arbitrage funds need to deal with it.

CBs commonly come with a single conversion price, but sometimes we see CBs with multiple conversion prices that are based on the underlying share price levels. Recall that CBs are generally issued by corporations whose intent is to have the CBs converted in the future. The reason for establishing multiple conversion prices, therefore, is to encourage future conversions.

If the new conversion price is to be set higher than the original conversion price, since a higher conversion price entails fewer shares to be issued upon conversion, the holders of the CB will be prompted to convert before the new conversion price goes into effect. Conversely, the new conversion price is typically set lower when the share price performance is poor. The lower conversion price will give CB investors, who could not convert at the original conversion price, the chance to convert at the new conversion price.

Obviously, the conversion price cannot be indefinitely reset to lower levels. If the conversion price is reset too low, an enormous number of shares will be issued upon conversion, which drives the share price even lower. Accordingly, the reset of the conversion price usually comes with a lower limit, the limit commonly accompanied by the mandatory conversion clause.

The mandatory conversion clause literally requires conversion to take place at some given time. What will happen if the share price keeps on going down beyond the mandatory conversion price? For CB investors, this is akin to holding a put option short.

Investors who are short put, for example, if the strike is at JPY100 and the share price is at JPY50, need to buy the JPY50 shares at JPY100. A way to avoid the potential loss incurred is to hedge the short-put position, and the hedge will be the opposite of that for a long option position (i.e., stocks are sold when the share price goes down and stocks are bought when the share price goes up). Clearly, the process generally increases volatility.

The manifestation of this process became most prominent in Japan during the financial crisis of 1998. Many Japanese banks, in order to strengthen their financial base, had issued a large number of convertible preferred shares with the mandatory conversion clause.

As nonperforming loans of the Japanese banks came into focus again due to the crisis, the bank share prices took a hit. Convertible arbitrage funds, which held a significant portion of the convertible preferred shares, had probably never thought that the share price would drop to the levels where the mandatory conversion would be triggered.

As the long-call positions turned into short-puts, the funds were forced to sell shares for a δ hedge. The selling that invited more selling came to be known as the "death spiral," and the world came to realize the danger of option short hedge perhaps for the first time in history.

Inverse and Leveraged ETFs

We just saw the γ effect of the option short position potentially contributing to the increase in single stock or market volatility. Something similar to the option γ effect can actually take place outside options.

In recent years, financial instruments called ETFs have enlarged their presence in the market. ETFs stand for Exchange Traded Funds and denote funds traded in the exchange as though they are equities. There are many kinds of ETFs, but in view of their impact on the market, inverse and leveraged ETFs particularly deserve a mention.

Inverse ETFs are the ETFs whose price moves in the opposite direction to the price of the underlying asset of the ETFs. For example, the price of the Nikkei 225 inverse ETF falls 10% when the Nikkei 225 rises by 10%. Leveraged ETFs, on the other hand, move in the same direction with the underlying asset but with a leverage. For example, when the Nikkei 225 rises by 10%, the Nikkei 225 2x leveraged ETF will rise by 20%. In these cases, the question is what the ETF managers do.

When the Nikkei 225 rises by 10%, the holder of the 2x leveraged Nikkei 225 expects his or her asset value to rise by 20%. In other words, the manager of the ETF must purchase 20% of the asset linked to the

Nikkei 225. Conversely, if the Nikkei 225 falls by 10%, the manager needs to sell 20% of the asset linked to the index.

The process of "buying when the underlying asset price goes up and selling when it goes down" is indeed similar to the process of the option-short δ hedge, potentially leading to the γ effect. In addition, as with the case of the δ hedge, since the asset value is settled after the market close, the selling or buying becomes concentrated near the close. For the Nikkei 225 and TOPIX inverse and leveraged ETFs, the underlying assets traded are the futures. Compared with the total trading volume of Nikkei 225 and TOPIX, the ETF-related futures volumes are limited in quantity. Since the ETF-related trading is all done in the short period of time near the close, however, the impact becomes more exaggerated.

A "hedge" required for inverse ETFs is similar to that for leveraged ETFs (1x inverse hedge corresponds to 2x leveraged hedge). Let us assume that the size of the asset under management is 100. If the ETF is the 1x inverse index ETF, then the futures used for this structure are a negative 100 (short 100 futures). If the index rises by 10%, then the index will be 110, and the futures value will be a negative 110. The asset under management is now 90, so the futures needed for the "hedge" will be negative 90, so the asset manager needs to buy back 20 futures.

If the γ refers to the needed adjustment in the asset under management relative to a 1% move in the size of the underlying asset, then the leveraged and inverse ETF γ can be calculated by the following equation:

$$\gamma = (leverage \times (leverage - 1) \times managed\ asset\ size)/100$$

For inverse ETFs, 1x inverse corresponds to 2x leverage, and 2x inverse corresponds to 3x leverage, so these numbers should be substituted in the above equation to calculate the appropriate γ.

The list of Nikkei 225 and TOPIX ETFs is publicly available. As of September 2015, the largest ETF was the Nikkei 225 2x leveraged ETF (Security code: 1570) set up and managed by Nomura Asset Management. Since the ETF offered 2x the return of the Nikkei index, the popularity of this ETF skyrocketed, with its trading volume surpassing that of the Toyota stock, amounting to some 14% of the total equity trading volume in the Tokyo Stock Exchange.

The collapse of the Chinese equity market, which began in August 2015, generated a reversal of fortune for this ETF, however. The manager was forced to sell Nikkei futures, which in turn, added downward pressure on the Japanese equity market. Since that time, whenever the equity market goes up and down in a significant way, professional traders tend to focus on index inverse and leveraged ETFs.

Put/Call Ratio

Market participants often speak of the put/call ratio. The ratio, calculated by dividing the 5-day average trading volume of the exchange-traded put options by the same 5-day average of the call options, is commonly viewed as a measure of the market sentiment. If the put trading volume is larger than that of the call, option investors are believed to be more pessimistic about the market, and vice versa.

The trend in the exchange is likely mirrored in the over-the-counter market. As stated earlier, over-the-counter trades are hedged by brokers more often than not, and therefore, an augmentation of put-long positions implies the augmentation of the short-put γ effect, and an augmentation of call-long positions implies the same of the short-call γ effect. Needless to say, the impact depends on the size of the positions, but at least in theory, a rising put/call ratio suggests a rise in the downside market risk, and a falling put/call ratio suggests a rise in the upside market risk.

If this is the case, wisdom seems to dictate that we should be selling the Nikkei 225 futures whenever the Nikkei put/call ratio rises and buying the Nikkei 225 futures whenever the put/call ratio falls. As usual, the reality is not that simple. In fact, our experience tells us to do the opposite. This is a phenomenon akin to "buy on the dip," which means that the market is more likely to rebound after a big drop.

More concretely, let us look at the cases where the Nikkei put/call ratio jumped in the last 10 years. If we take the top 30 largest jumps, 53.3% of the time, the Nikkei 225 recorded a gain a week after. So, the result is about 50/50. Two weeks afterward, however, the number rises to 63.3%; a month after, 72.4%; and two months and three months after, 64.3%. In other words, at least probability tells us that a jump in the put/call ratio offers a good buying opportunity.

Once again, the key word is "probability." The gain recorded 64.3% of the time means that the returns are negative 35.7% of the time, which is a loss ratio of 1 out of 3, and the number may not be easily brushed off. What is important is to judge under what circumstances the put/call ratio has jumped and what caused the jump. It goes without saying that the judgment hinges on various factors, such as the macro environment, policy announcements, or other events.

The put/call ratio also has a close relation to the option skew. The option skew is the shape of the implied volatility curve, expressed simply, the spread between the implied volatility of the call option and the implied volatility of the put option. The spread is calculated by subtracting call option implied volatility above the strike (usually 5% to 10% above) from the put option implied volatility below the strike (usually 5% to 10% below), and is expressed as a percentage.

Stated another way, while the put/call ratio expresses the ratio of the traded volume, the skew expresses the difference between the put and call implied volatility. If the skew is large, puts are being bought more aggressively, which suggests increased concern on the downside, and if the skew is small, the contrary may be true. It is difficult to say which skew levels offer a clear buy or sell signal on the equity market. The skew simply reveals the views of option investors and probably depends on the market conditions of the time.

VIX Index

When we speak of volatility, we cannot avoid discussing the VIX Index (the "fear index"). The VIX Index was developed by the CBOE (Chicago Board Options Exchange) to measure the future volatility of the S&P 500 and is calculated from the volatility attained from the collection of S&P 500 option prices.

The actual formula is complicated and replicating it in this literature offers no merit, but we can think of it as the volatility calculated from 30-day S&P 500 options with various strikes. In other words, the VIX Index expresses the implied volatility of the broad market (i.e., expected near-future volatility of the S&P 500).

If this index is high, at least option traders are expecting the future market volatility to be high, and vice versa. The higher the expected future volatility, the higher the expected rate of future market fluctuation, and as discussed earlier, since the market tends to display higher volatility when it goes down, the name "fear index" was coined. With this premise, can we say that the equity market is a "sell" when the VIX Index spikes up? The answer, again, is "not necessarily."

In September 2008, Lehman Brothers filed for Chapter 11, ending its long corporate history and, at the same time, inadvertently becoming the symbol of the global financial crisis. The VIX Index was accused at the time of failing to "foresee" this significant event.

As elaborated in the "Historical and Implied" section above, we seldom see implied volatility rise before historical does. In other words, implied volatility spikes only after the market plummets. What this fact suggests is that when the implied volatility jumps, it is often "too late." This is not hard to understand, since if option traders could foresee the market collapse before it takes place, they might as well trade their own funds rather than working for brokers or hedge funds.

Indeed, we see many occasions where the market rebounds after a sharp rise in volatility, implying that had we sold the market (via selling index futures) after the VIX Index spikes, we could have suffered a substantial loss. If this is the case, then, should we hold on to the market in the face of sharp jumps in the VIX Index? The answer, obviously, depends on how long we should hold on to the market and which stocks we should retain.

The collapse of Lehman Brothers in September 2008 and events that took place in the following days took the VIX Index to a new high, and the tumultuous market saw no end until March of 2009. Still, this is nothing but an afterthought. The fact of the matter is that no one knew at the

FIGURE 3.1 VIX since 1990

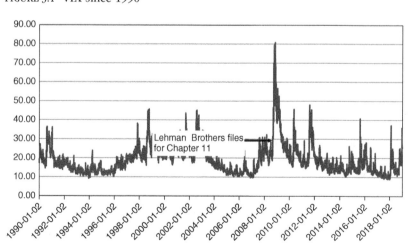

Data Source: FRED

time that the global financial crisis would end (in a way, it did not, as the subsequent Euro crises suggest). Probably it would have been best not to own any stocks during those times, and if we had to own stocks, we should have just stuck to defensive stocks such as those in the food, pharmaceutical, railway, and utility sectors.

Where the above discussion leads is that we should probably not automatically turn buyers of the market after a sharp rise in the VIX Index, and the converse is also probably true. What we may say, however, is that low volatility generally means market complacency and low inter-stock correlations and, thus, does not last indefinitely.

Also, as stated in the "Volatility" section above, volatility tends to mean-revert and hence never becomes zero as long as the market is alive. In other words, if the volatility is falling in an up market, the market will necessarily go down, and in the down market, the market will necessarily go up. Forecasting the exact timing of rebounds or downturns is not easy, but by looking at the market as a whole (economy, FX, and interest rates, for example), we can guesstimate which way the market is headed and prepare for the upcoming changes.

As alluded to in the "GPIF" section in Chapter 2, we have seen occurrences of global shifts of funds triggered by the spikes in the VIX Index. It is not surprising to see active portfolio managers taking actions based upon the levels of the VIX Index. Nor is it surprising to see program trading that includes the VIX Index or some other measures of market risk in its algorithm.

If the majority of the market participants are utilizing the same or similar measures or rules, the market will move by them. The likelihood of one of the measures being the VIX Index or another measure of volatility is quite high, and therefore when the VIX Index spikes up, shifting to defensive stocks, such as high-dividend-yield stocks, might be wise.

We may note, however, that in judging when to move back to growth or value stocks from defensive ones, neither the VIX nor other measures of volatility are very useful. When the VIX Index spikes up, chances are that it will come down in a matter of days, but we may not want to abandon our defensive posture.

The VIX Index spikes up for a reason, and even when it comes down, often the "reason" still exists. The history of the VIX Index or other market volatility indices tells us that spikes tend to occur in a cluster. When, then, can we turn from defense to offense? The discussion is left to the next chapter.

CHAPTER 4

Market Tops and Bottoms

E xperience tells us that guessing the top of the market is far easier than guessing the bottom of it. The market top usually shows up after a long climb. Of course, there is no clear definition as to how long the "long" should be. We could say, however, that when the market climbs to the top, various indicators begin to signal "overheat," and at least for some short duration, and sometimes for some considerable duration, the market experiences a correction.

In contrast, even when "oversold" signals flash and we see temporary rebounds, in many cases the market will continue to correct. We may say that here again, human psyche is at work.

As the phrase "profit take" suggests, when we achieve certain returns (out of greed), fear begins to grip our soul. This is the first reason for a market correction. And once the correction begins, the fear amplifies, and unless investors see clear signals, they tend to stay away from the market. This may be the primary reason why it is difficult to guess the bottom of the market.

For humans, it may be easier to eradicate greed than fear. In this chapter, we will consider a few indicators that may tell us the top and bottom of the market, as we continue to struggle with greed and fear.

Volatility as Indicator

When the equity market rises steadily, after a while the market volatility drops to a level not seen or seldom seen in the past. This is a danger signal, and we may wish to check futures open interest levels and cash arbitrage positions, in addition to various technical indicators, to be discussed later. Although there are no "absolute" levels for these indicators, we can at least make a probabilistic judgment from historical examples.

If, after a long ascent of the market, we see significant policy announcements, clear signs of a weakening economy, or large movements in interest rates or FX, there is a good chance of a market crash, and we need to be extra cautious in these cases. As an action plan, it may prove prudent to take a profit and shift funds to more defensive stocks. Defensive stocks are typically those with low historical volatility, and in terms of sectors, generally belong to the food, telecom, utility, and railway sectors.

In recent years, we hear a lot about hedge funds such as commodity trading advisor (CTA) funds and risk parity funds. In contrast with CTA funds, which are basically momentum funds that follow a trend, risk parity funds place volatility in their core strategy (these categorizations are oversimplified for our discussion purposes).

Risk parity funds commonly practice diversification by investing globally in equities, commodities, and bonds, and their strategy is to move their funds from high volatility assets to low volatility assets. They abhor high volatility, and as soon as volatility begins to rise, shift funds, but as touched upon in the "GPIF" section in Chapter 2, there are some equity-only funds that follow similar investment disciplines.

These funds utilize various technical indicators to forecast future market volatility, and one of the indicators is likely a volatility level far from the historical average. Here, market volatility refers to the volatility of major equity indices such as the Nikkei 225 and TOPIX.

There are a few reasons why the market volatility drops. One is a fall in volatility of each index-constituent stock, and another reason is a fall in the correlation among constituent stocks, or both. That a fall in correlation causes a drop in market volatility is easy to understand: if the index consists of just two equally-weighted stocks, A and B, and if A goes up by 5% and B comes down by 5%, the index will not move (strictly, the index will move somewhat due to the change in weight), and the index volatility on that day will be 0%.

Ordinarily, an index consists of many stocks, and they move by different percentage points. If the correlation is +1, all the stocks moved in the same direction by the same percentage. If the correlation is –1, an equal number of stocks moved in the opposite direction by the same percentage. In actuality, the correlation fluctuates between +1 and –1. And with other conditions kept constant, the higher the correlation, the higher the index volatility, and vice versa.

As noted in the "Put/Call Ratio" section in Chapter 3, a volatility spike can be used as a "buy-on-the-dip" opportunity, but the returns are not necessarily spectacular and the win-ratio is contingent on market sentiment. This is because, as discussed in the "VIX Index" section in Chapter 3, particularly when the economy is in deterioration, volatility spikes tend to occur in succession.

While a difficulty in calculation makes it less usable, a more reliable "buy-on-the-dip" signal is the correlation coefficient. This may be due to the fact that the correlation moves between +1 and –1 and tends to

TABLE 4.1 Nikkei 225 return after correlation spikes

	10D Return	20D Return	3M Return
Average	0.70%	2.50%	4.90%
Stdv	6.50%	4.40%	6.90%
Win Ratio	66.70%	72.20%	77.80%

Source: FRED

mean-revert more than the volatility. Table 4.1 lists the 10-day, 20-day, and 3-month Nikkei 225 index returns when the Nikkei 225 was bought with the signal of its 1-month "realized correlation" rising above the 1.5σ of the 6-month average.

The above statistics are based on the data sample from 2003 to 2009, but the "win ratio" is largely unchanged whether the market was tending upward or downward. Unfortunately, the "realized correlation" is not something readily available to ordinary investors and thus its practical usage as a signal may be limited.

Also, we note that Table 4.1 only refers to the case where the correlation rose to 1.5σ or above, and we do not vouch for equivalent results when the correlation falls. In other words, using the correlation as a "sell" signal may not be a valid strategy.

This said, stocks do not perennially move with negative correlations, meaning that probability dictates that a negative correlation cannot last forever. If that is the case, what reverses low correlation and makes stocks begin to move more or less in the same direction?

Economy and Policy as Indicators

A terrorist attack such as 9/11 or a major natural disaster such as the Great East Japan Earthquake inevitably sinks the market, but since these events are unpredictable, we will not take them into consideration. Apart from these events, one of the major elements that drive the market in one direction is the state of the economy.

As described earlier, our experience tells us that to know the state of the economy, we only need to follow a few crucial leading indicators. We have mentioned that these indicators include the ISMPMI and the OECD CLI. When these indicators show signs of sudden deterioration, we are almost certain to see the elevation of market volatility.

Whether we can use these indicators to see where the economy is going before their official release of data, we claimed for the OECD CLI in the "More on OECD CLI" section in Chapter 1, that forecasting was possible to some extent by isolating the country-by-country constituents and their respective weights. For the ISMPMI, we should remember that the indicator is based on a survey.

If manufacturers believe that the economy is on the mend, they will likely increase capital expenditure and inventory, but if they believe the opposite, they will likely refrain from additional investments and may even lower prices to reduce inventory. All of these corporate behaviors directly impact the ISMPMI. When corporate heads see the worsening economic indicators, they generally further rein in their investments. This is the "downward spiral" mechanism.

Of course, in reality, there are as many corporate heads as there are numbers of corporations, and what they see and think are not necessarily uniform. Undoubtedly, however, they are a group of learned and experienced individuals who share a certain common sense, and when the common sense becomes the consensus, corporate activities may dwindle or resurge.

One such commonsense response may be formed around the policy and action of the central bank. As written in "The Fed" section in Chapter 2, since the central bank acts to stabilize the economy, if the action is deemed to destabilize the economy contrary to the intent, corporations will be more cautious regarding their future outlook and activities.

While the Fed's role is to "stabilize the economy," history shows that the Fed's job has largely been that of fighting inflation. Indeed, fighting inflation has been the job of the world's central banks.

Deflation is an offspring of recession and thus has existed long into the past, but the word "deflation" did not become part of the household lexicon until about twenty years ago, and as far as I know, the epicenter was Japan. Thus began the anti-deflation measures by the BoJ, followed by the Fed and ECB post-2008, only to be expanded into Kuroda Bazooka, as discussed in the "Abenomics" section in Chapter 2.

Returning to the Fed, since the Fed has historically been an inflation fighter, its main duty is that of braking the economy. Inflation may simmer down when a brake is applied to the economy, but the economy may also come to a grinding halt as a result.

The BoJ's interest rate policy contributed to the collapse of the '80s bubble in Japan, for example. Similarly, it is easy to imagine how the Fed's interest rate policy contributed to the collapse of the internet bubble in 2000 and the credit bubble in 2008. A recent example may be the Fed rate hike in December 2015. Whether we look at the GDP growth rate, durable goods new orders, housing starts, or the ISMPMI, the US economy was not strong enough to absorb the impact of the rate hike. Unsurprisingly, coinciding with the timing of the Fed rate hike, global equity markets began to crumble. The initial reaction was mild, but as the December ISMPMI showed a sudden and substantial decline, the equity market came tumbling down. This was particularly apparent in Japan.

These examples suggest that in passing judgment on market tops, we must ponder the balance between the state of the economy and the level of the market. If the market is believed to be lagging the economy, the market will continue to rise, and vice versa. When the market is not overheated and, at the same time, the economy is robust, even in the wake of rate hikes by the central bank, the market will likely remain strong.

In addition to the human psyche element, a difficulty in guessing the bottom of the market arises because the bottom often does not hinge on the state of the economy. A simple example involving the rate of unemployment, a frequently quoted statistic, may aid in understanding this.

While it somewhat differs from country to country, generally full employment is deemed achieved when the rate of unemployment is somewhere around 3% or 4%. In other words, an economy will not improve much more from these unemployment levels, and the top of the market is likely close at hand.

When we think of the bottom of the market, however, there is no clear unemployment level that signals it. Needless to say, the unemployment level will never reach 100%, but this is an extreme case. The problem is that there is no historical answer as to what rate of unemployment foretells the bottom of the market. In other words, whatever the rate of unemployment may be, the market can rebound, the onset of which forms the bottom of the market.

In most cases, the market does not rebound due to a sudden improvement in economic statistics. Rather, the market rebounds due to policy announcements designed to improve the economy or due to technical factors discussed later. Only insiders know when and what policy will be announced. This is just another source of the difficulty in guessing the bottom of the market.

It generally takes months or even years for a given economic policy to impact the real economy. Accordingly, when a policy is announced, the market is not responding to an actual improvement in the economy but the content of the policy and expectation of the policy's impact. Whether the resulting market rebound becomes sustainable depends on the actual improvement in the economy. That said, although it may take months before the policy reveals its impact, the harbinger of the impact may show much sooner, and even if it does not, often it is wise to invest in equities assuming the effectiveness of the policy.

The reason, again, is that corporations and investors often share a common thought. When the central bank cuts interest rates and engages in quantitative easing, or when the government announces a large-scale supplementary budget to stimulate the economy, corporations, believing that the economy will improve, are likely to increase spending (i.e., they may increase capital expenditure or hire more workers).

Investors, too, may decide to increase equity holdings or buy real estate even on borrowed money, and ordinary citizens, attracted by a favorable interest rate environment, may decide to buy housing units or luxury items. All these activities pile onto each other to boost the economy, forming something opposite to the "death spiral." This is not just an economic theory but is a phenomenon that happens in front of our very eyes.

In using the state of the economy as a yardstick for the top and bottom of the market, a measure often quoted is the Buffett Indicator. The name springs from the famed US investor Warren Buffett, and the ratio is a quotient of the total equity market capitalization divided by the nation's GDP. If in the US, the equity market capitalization is that of the S&P 500, and if in Japan, TOPIX, and the GDP should be the inflation-reflecting nominal GDP.

The usefulness of this ratio arises from history, as the collapse of major "bubbles" in the past was triggered when the Buffett Indicator was either above or close to 1. Also, the market, after collapse, tended to find a bottom when this ratio was close to 0.5. The usefulness of this ratio is limited, however, by the scarcity of such examples (i.e., the Buffett Indicator has seldom gone above 1 or below 0.5).

Additionally, even when the ratio goes beyond 1, the condition can last for quite some time. Good examples of this can be seen in the recent equity market in the US and in Japan. As of November 2017, the US equity market has been shifting above the Buffett Indicator of 1 for a few years, and the Japanese equity market for at least several months.

Valuations and Technical Indicators

So far, we have considered the ways to forecast peaks and troughs of the market from the viewpoints of volatility, the economy, and policies. In this section, we will look into more traditional methods, use of valuations and technical indicators. Having said this, the realm of valuations and technical measures is broad and deep so that we cannot possibly cover the entirety of these subjects in this book, and perhaps moreover, unless history repeats itself 100%, examining every minute detail and situation where these factors were relevant in the past may not be all that helpful. Accordingly, we will limit our discussion to more or less representative and well-known valuation and technical measures.

We note that while economic indicators and policy responses may be more suitable in forecasting a mid- to long-term stock market movement, valuations and technical indicators are more often used for short-term predictions. The success of the OECD CLI may be impressive, but, as discussed earlier, this indicator is more suited for forecasting mid- to long-term trends of the equity market. Valuations and technical indicators, therefore, can possibly compensate for any defects of the longer-term economic indicators.

One area of technical indicators is the chart. There are those analysts and traders called chartists, who employ shapes of the market movements (charts) in timing the market. They not only observe the shapes and trends of the market but also often utilize various technical measures as well. I am a complete stranger in understanding the shapes and forms of charts, and thus have no credibility in commenting on the validity of the subject.

Warren Buffett apparently pays little attention to charts, stating that they look the same when turned upside down, but he is a quintessential fundamental long-term investor and has no need to understand short-term fluctuations of the market.

There are, however, day-traders who anecdotally have claimed to amass considerable wealth by effective usage of charts. As always, if a large group of people see the same phenomenon and move in the same way, stocks and stock markets will move. In this sense, charts cannot be easily dispensed with as "nonsense," but whether their validity depends on something more than a beauty pageant can be debated.

If historical investor returns are anywhere near normal distribution, then there should be those that boast outstanding returns almost consistently, and it is possible that those investors might have been simply "lucky." Whatever the case may be, my own ignorance on the subject means that I cannot discuss the validity of their methods. What can be said is that the validity may be evidenced by the simple existence of those who have claimed to benefit from charts.

Valuations generally refer to those traditional measures, such as P/B (price-to-book ratio), P/E (price-to-earnings ratio), and EV/EBITDA (enterprise value/earnings before interest, taxes, depreciation, and amortization). These measures are used to judge whether the share price is cheap or expensive relative to the fundamentals.

Apart from the extremes, there is no definite and absolute fair value of these measures. Depending on the market sentiment, and for single stocks, their historical valuations and valuations of their peers, fair values are determined. Once again, the beauty pageant aspect of the stock market asserts itself here.

Can, then, these valuation measures tell us where to find the top and bottom of the equity market? If valuations are the beauty pageant tools, then the answer seems to be yes, but historical examination tells us that this is not necessarily so. Said another way, investors can suffer a great loss, at least in the short-term, if they pass judgment on market tops or bottoms by using valuation measures alone (mid- to long-term effectiveness will be discussed later).

We often hear an argument that P/B = 1 is the bottom price, whether for the entire market or single stocks. The textbook argument goes this way: since the "B" of P/B is the book value, the share price cannot theoretically fall below its book value. This argument, however, overlooks the fluctuation in the book value. When the market collapses, often the book value itself suffers a great deal of damage.

In the fall of 2008, during the middle of the global financial crisis, some argued that since the TOPIX P/B fell below 1, the Japanese equity market was a "buy." Needless to say, the market kept on falling afterward, and had we followed the above advice, the trade would have incurred a loss at least for months to come.

We may think that if the share price and book value fall alike, the P/B measure may still prove effective. The problem is that while the share price changes are monitored and observed constantly, the book value can only be known by company disclosure and generally is kept under a veil until the time for company reports. The P/B's falling below 1 is a phenomenon that takes place because investors assume before disclosure that the book value has already suffered impairment.

A similar situation can be said of P/E and EV/EBITDA. In calculating P/E or EV/EBITDA, a common practice is to use estimated future earnings numbers for the denominator "E." Take a company whose fiscal year-end falls at the end of March, for example. If "now" is September 2017, the earnings number to be used is the forecast number as of March 2018, and the forecast number comes either from industry analysts of brokerage firms or fund managers, or their consensus.

Analysts typically form their views based upon company forecasts. In general, the views are not renewed frequently but every quarter or even with less periodicity. When the economy shows sudden weakness (which can trigger or be caused by an equity market collapse), company forecasts and analyst views are often unable to keep up with the sudden change, and thus P/E or EV/EBITDA becomes unsuitable in predicting the market bottom.

Here, we looked at 2008, a very special year, as an example, but whenever we have seen major market collapses, similar phenomena existed. As it is difficult to use valuations to detect market bottoms, it is also difficult to use valuations to detect market tops, since the same issues with the book value and the forecast earnings still exist when the market is strong.

To test all existing technical indicators under all conceivable circumstances is not feasible. The argument here, therefore, will be once again limited. Suffice it to say that as far as my experience goes, I have never met a trader who was perennially successful by simply following technical indicators. In this regard, the usefulness of technical indicators is probably also limited.

A difficulty with technical indicators is that even for a single indicator, many versions exist, and they need to be selectively used depending on market conditions and prevailing sentiments. Moreover, even the selective usage does not guarantee a positive outcome, and more effective usage may need to wait for the completion of AI as the trading tool. With these understandings, let us now look at the more popular technical indicators: RSI, Bollinger Bands, and Toraku ratio.

RSI (relative strength index) is a ratio between the rate of upside price moves and downside price moves in a given period of time. It offers a way to quantify "oversold" and "overbought" conditions. When this indicator is below 25–20, it signals a "buy," and when above 70–80, it signals a "sell." RSI is expressed by the following equation:

$$RSI = Average\ rate\ of\ upside\ price\ moves\ in\ a\ period/$$
$$(Average\ rate\ of\ upside\ price\ moves\ in\ a\ period$$
$$+\ Average\ rate\ of\ downside\ price\ moves\ in\ a\ period) \times 100$$

At a glance, RSI appears to be an effective tool. Indeed, equity prices and indices tend to bounce up when RSI is close to or below 20 and fall after RSI's climb close to or above 80.

The problem is that equity prices and indices often bounce up long before RSI gets close to or below 20 and turn down well below RSI = 80. Also, there is no clear answer as to how long we need to hold the equities or indices after purchase at RSI = 20. Even if we conduct an extensive examination of the subject, the likelihood is that the answer varies widely, depending on market conditions.

Other outstanding issues may include the occasional cases where stocks or indices continue to rise after RSI reaches 80 or fall after RSI reaches 20. The obvious implication is that strictly obeying RSI as the buy-sell indicator may put us on the short end of the stick. Additionally, the definition of RSI leaves "a period" uncertain. Commonly, a period of 14 days or 25 days is used, but we do not know if these periods are ideal. Once again, the "ideal" period likely depends on market conditions and sentiments.

Needless to say, RSI is a statistical measure, and therefore, we expect occasional misses. Accordingly, we may be tempted simply to follow the "buy-at-RSI=20 and sell-at-RSI=80" strategy. A backtest of this strategy, however, did not generate a positive return either consistently or over the long term.

Bollinger Bands are similar to RSI in principle. The approach takes the standard deviation of the price history to set up the upper and lower limits. The buy or sell signal will be lit when these limits are breached.

This approach assumes that the historical prices are normally distributed. The standard deviation is expressed as σ, as noted earlier, where 1σ indicates that 68% of the prices and 2σ indicates that 95% of the prices are contained within that range in a given period.

For 2σ Bollinger Bands, for example, if the price goes above the upper band, since such an occurrence was observed only 2% of the time in a given period, the event is considered rare and unlikely to last long. In this case, therefore, a "sell" signal will be lit. If the price falls below the lower Bollinger Band, on the other hand, a "buy" signal will be lit.

When we look at the actual price movement, we indeed see the price fluctuating between the upper and lower bands. This is not surprising since the data is based on the past and is expected from the definition of Bollinger Bands.

Just as the Bollinger Bands principle is similar to that of RSI, so are the problems. First and foremost, there is uncertainty as to what "period" is the appropriate period in which the standard deviations are to be taken. At the threshold of a strong bull or bear market, in particular, a given period in the recent past may not function at all.

There is also uncertainty associated with the level of the σ. That is, determining whether 2σ or 1.5σ or some other σ is appropriate depends on the market conditions of the time. Once again, to identify which level of σ is appropriate under given market conditions, we may need the help of AI. At present, the best we can do is to conduct as thorough a backtest as possible and come up with some σ based on the resulting statistics.

Under the assumption that the past price pattern will be repeated in the future, the Bollinger Bands approach is a valid one and may prove to be effective. Of course, if future price patterns deviate widely from the past ones, the Bollinger Bands approach may result in catastrophe.

The Toraku ratio has been in use for many decades and has many followers. The ratio, unlike RSI and Bollinger Bands, cannot be applied to single stocks. Rather, it is used to judge how "overheated" or "overcooled" the market is. The Toraku ratio also depends on the measurement period. The 25-day Toraku ratio, for example, is expressed by the following formula:

Toraku Ratio = (Number of advancers in 25 days/
Number of decliners in 25 days) × 100

TABLE 4.2 Toraku ratio backtest

Level	5D Return				10D Return			
	120	**130**	**70**	**60**	**120**	**130**	**70**	**60**
Average	−0.20%	0.10%	−0.70%	4.20%	−0.50%	0.90%	−0.50%	4.60%
Stdev	2.20%	2.30%	5.00%	8.90%	3.30%	3.70%	5.20%	9.90%

Source: TSE

Commonly, a Toraku ratio above 120–130 represents an "overheated" market and below 70–60 represents an "overcooled" market. Table 4.2 is the backtest result of trading the TOPIX following these measures over the last ten years (using the 25-day Toraku ratio):

The effectiveness of the Toraku ratio is particularly apparent as a "buy-on-the-dip" measure, after the ratio falls below 60 (although the standard deviation is large). Also notable is that the effectiveness largely disappears after 5 days (the difference is small between 5- and 10-day returns), confirming that the Toraku ratio is a short-term measure.

Nevertheless, though the Toraku ratio may serve as a measure of the overheated and overcooled markets, it may not be all that effective, on the average, as an inflection point measure.

So far, we have seen limited success in capturing the short-term fluctuation of the market by valuation or technical measures alone. As discussed in the "VIX Index" section in Chapter 3, the situation where the VIX Index spikes up (valuation and technical measures collapse) leads to investor abhorrence of risk and tendency to switch into more defensive stocks. This inclination suggests favoring of more bond-like stocks or selling of stocks against bonds.

Also, judging from the Toraku ratio and other measures, the "buy-on-the-dip" strategy does appear to work at least partially. It is a question of probability, of course, but extreme cases in the past, in particular, behoove us to consider the "buy-on-the-dip" strategy.

On February 12, 2016, the Nikkei 225 Index dropped over 12% from its 25-day moving average. The index bounced up 7.2% the next day, and a week after was still up 6.8%; two weeks after, up 8.3%; and after one month, up 13.3% from the February 12 close level.

Similar cases, where the Nikkei 225 Index fell more than 12% from its 25-day moving average, have taken place 27 times since 1990, excluding the February 12, 2016, example. Some 63% of these cases are concentrated in October 2008, which makes the period indeed extraordinary. If we exclude this period from our backtest, the average return 1 day after the decline is 2.5%, with a 90% win ratio; the average return 1 week after is 4.6%, win ratio 100%; 2 weeks after, 4.3% and 90%; and 1 month after, 6.9% and 90%, suggesting that the "buy-on-the-dip" strategy was the correct one.

Similar statistics can be collected by ranking the 1-day percentage decline of the Nikkei 225 Index. The data is somewhat old, starting from May 22, 2013, but if we collect all the cases where the Nikkei 225 fell more than 5% in a day since 1990, the average return after 1 day is 1.3% with a 71% win ratio; after 1 week, 3.4% and 71%; and after 1 month, 3.5% and 70%. These are all decent statistics, although not as good as the earlier cases probably because this backtest does not exclude October 2008.

These examples may suggest that, even when using technical measures and the VIX Index as inflection point indicators rather than judging from commonly accepted levels, we probably should look at more extreme levels. Needless to say, extreme cases do not happen too often, but market tops and bottoms are indeed those rare cases, and our argument here is simply to examine which measures are the most effective.

In this regard, we should note that although, as discussed earlier, the valuation measures such as P/B and P/E, with book values and forecast earnings subject to change, may not be effective in the short term, they can yet prove their validity when technical considerations are added.

Table 4.3 represents the backtest results of trading the TOPIX when the TOPIX P/E and P/B were either below or above their 7-year average. The backtest assumes that the TOPIX futures had been bought when the P/E or P/B was below the 7-year average and sold when it was above the 7-year average, and it measures the 3-month, 6-month, 1-year, 2-year, and 3-year returns afterwards. The CAPE notation in the table refers to the cyclically adjusted price-to-earnings ratio, which uses the 10-year average earnings figures in the denominator of the P/E to avoid the annual fluctuation in earnings.

More strictly, the CAPE calculation needs to take inflation into account, but since inflation has been virtually nonexistent in Japan over the last ten years, this factor is ignored in the present case for the sake of simplicity. The "Nonadjusted P/E" in the table, on the other hand,

TABLE 4.3 Trading TOPIX by 7-year average P/E and
P/B (since Sept 2010)

	CAPE				
	3M	**6M**	**1Y**	**2Y**	**3Y**
Average	2.0%	3.1%	8.6%	30.1%	58.5%
Median	1.4%	2.8%	5.6%	37.7%	56.6%
Stdv	9.9%	16.0%	25.6%	31.3%	35.9%
	Nonadjusted P/E				
Average	2.5%	4.7%	13.3%	33.6%	58.1%
Median	2.8%	3.3%	10.7%	37.7%	56.6%
Stdv	9.8%	15.6%	23.5%	27.5%	36.6%
	P/B				
Average	2.3%	3.5%	8.9%	26.3%	56.7%
Median	1.9%	3.1%	4.5%	35.0%	56.2%
Stdv	10.1%	15.9%	25.5%	33.7%	38.6%

Source: TSE

denotes the ordinary P/E, which uses the single-year earnings in the denominator.

The reason the 7-year average is being used is simply due to the lack of data. In fact, using the 5-year average instead of the 7-year average generates results not too distinct from Table 4.3. What Table 4.3 shows is that the CAPE, P/E, and P/B all have a tendency to return to their long-term average. It is this tendency that generates the profit when any one of these valuation measures deviates from its average.

As usual, the reality is not as simple as it sounds, however. Looked at closely, the standard deviation of each return is quite high, with the possible exception of the 3-year return. If we assume that the returns are normally distributed, probability dictates that the returns could have been negative. (For example, the 3-month return of the CAPE case could have ranged from -7.9% to +11.9% with a 68% probability.)

If the 3-year return is an exception, maybe we should wait for 3 years, but again, the results differ depending upon the period of observation. Table 4.3 is the backtest results obtained since September 2010.

TABLE 4.4 Trading TOPIX by 7-year Average P/B
(since May 1998)

	P/B				
	3M	**6M**	**1Y**	**2Y**	**3Y**
Average	0.7%	2.2%	5.3%	18.2%	29.4%
Median	0.6%	2.6%	2.4%	21.1%	39.7%
Stdev	10.4%	15.9%	23.5%	32.4%	39.7%

Source: TSE

The equity market was largely upward-sloping after the global financial crisis and benefiting from Abenomics.

Table 4.4 represents the backtest results since May 1998 (due to the lack of data, only the P/B was backtested). The 2-year and 3-year returns are once again attractive but nevertheless substantially below those obtained earlier.

CHAPTER 5

Other Market Movers

Foreign Investors

The Tokyo Stock Exchange homepage lists the weekly statistics of investor activities, detailing which category of investors, such as retail, domestic corporate, and foreign, bought or sold Japanese equities. Retail investors can be a powerful entity, particularly for small stocks, and domestic corporate investors can assert their presence, as we saw in the "GPIF" section in Chapter 2.

In Japanese equities, however, the most influential bar none are the foreign investors. To this date, about two-thirds of the total equity trading volume comes from foreign investors, but their investment style also contributes to their significance.

As there are many types of domestic corporate investors, there are many types of foreign investors as well. Painting with a broad brush, however, foreign investors can be divided into two groups: pension funds and hedge funds. Some pension funds invest in hedge funds and thus they are not necessarily mutually exclusive, and hedge funds are not all alike, but those are minor distinctions in the present argument.

I have spent about a quarter century in the field of equity investment, four years working for one of the largest US public pension funds. The management of the funds at that time was done almost 100% in-house, with a handful of specialized portfolio managers in charge of their country and regional equity portfolios. Similar structures exist to this day, and other public pension funds are not too different.

The investment style was top-down, from macro to micro, meaning that first, asset allocation was decided, followed by country or regional allocation, sector allocation, and finally individual stock selection. Asset allocation refers to the process whereby funds are allocated to particular assets, such as equities and bonds. This process was outsourced to an organization that looked after a large number of US public pension funds, and the decision was made annually.

In the section "More on OECD CLI" in Chapter 1, we saw that more than 50% of US pension fund assets are in equities. Indeed, the pension fund I worked for perennially had 60%–70% of its assets in equities. I was initially doubtful of this asset allocation in the midst of the internet bubble collapse, but viewed long-term, the strategy turned out to be successful.

Country or regional allocation refers to which country or region in the global context the funds are to be allocated to. For this decision, macro factors, such as politics and economy, and more micro factors, such as corporate governance, market trends, and overall valuations, needed to be considered.

This decision was administered in-house, where the portfolio managers met and discussed their ideas and suggestions on a quarterly basis unless the market environment was in rapid change, in which case the decisions were made more often than quarterly. After taking into account various options, the final country and regional asset allocation decisions were deferred to the director of the equity investment division.

Sector allocation and individual stock selection were left to the discretion of the portfolio managers. Their job was to outperform the index (e.g., the MSCI Japan Index) by managing the portfolios they constructed within the limit of prescribed risk-tolerance levels.

Described above is the general process of asset allocation by pension funds, but hedge funds that manage money globally are likely to have a similar investment style. By now it is perhaps clear why foreign investors have a major influence in the Japanese equity market: when they make country asset allocation decisions, they move a large sum of funds in and out of the country. If they are positive on Japanese equities, money is injected, and if they turn negative, money is taken out. The market moves up and down accordingly.

In contrast, Japanese domestic corporate investors affect the equity market in the opposite way. For Japanese domestic corporate investors, what constitutes country asset allocation for foreign investors is actually asset allocation. Typically, the asset allocation decisions are made annually or even less frequently, and the percentages of assets allocated to equities, bonds, or other asset classes are fixed at that time.

When the equity market rises, the percentage weight allocated to equities will be exceeded. Domestic corporate investors, as a result, will be forced to sell equities. Likewise, when the equity market falls, the opposite action will be taken.

This is the reason why foreign investors are often said to be market movers and domestic corporate investors are often said to be market stabilizers. Foreign investors move the equity market, thereby contributing to an increase in market volatility, while domestic corporate investors stabilize the equity market, inadvertently contributing to a decrease in market volatility.

When we compare the Nikkei 225 moves during the market open hours and overnight (the Nikkei 225 futures market is open in the US), we see that most of the moves come from overnight (in other words, the moves between the close and next-day open of the equity market in Japan). This fact alone suggests the importance of foreign investors in the Japanese equity market.

How, then, can we profit from foreign investors, investors so influential in the Japanese equity market? In fact, the essence of this book could be condensed into this very question in a way.

As described earlier, foreign investors come in all shapes and forms, all of which, by their sheer trading volume, contribute to and influence the inflection points of the market. Their investment styles, of course, have close connections to many of the themes covered in this book.

In "More on OECD CLI" in Chapter 1, we discovered that the fluctuation in the OECD CLI has high correlation with the activity of foreign investors. To wit, foreign investors, in general, are quite conscious of macro environments. It inevitably follows that foreign investors pay close attention to policy decisions as well, since policy decisions often gravely affect the economy.

In the "VIX Index" section in Chapter 3, we also saw the close connection between rising market volatility and the flow of global funds. Risk-parity funds are types of hedge funds that use volatility as their chief risk measure. For them, high volatility is the very signal that prompts shifting of funds from high- to low-volatility instruments.

Of course, foreign investors are not always right, as the failure of countless hedge funds over the years demonstrates. To follow foreign investors may not be the best advice at all times, but once again, the equity market is a beauty pageant, and if a large sum of money moves in one direction, the market moves as well.

In view of stock selections, the foreign stock ownership ratio may serve as useful information. The foreign stock ownership ratio is the data provided by corporations in Japan in their annual company reports. By comparing the present numbers to past ones, we may be able to fathom, to some extent, just what drives foreigners to buy or sell particular stocks.

When the global economy falters, Japanese equities usually go underweight and remain there in most investment portfolios. Under this circumstance, stocks in the TOPIX Core 30 Index and other blue-chip names have often been sold off by foreign investors. Accordingly, if any signs of economic recovery are detected, or the BoJ engages in QE (quantitative easing), or any other positive impact is expected in the near future, we, as a rule, should be purchasing those stocks first and foremost.

Indeed, viewed yearly, there is a positive correlation between the change in the share price and the change in the foreign ownership ratio. Needless to say, however, the foreign ownership ratio is not the only factor that moves the equity price, and other factors need to be taken into account before making investment decisions.

Factor Analysis

Institutional investors typically isolate factors to discriminate and assign weights accordingly to the stocks in their portfolios, as the market condition changes. Recall that the goal for most institutional investors is to outperform a given index without too much deviation (keeping the tracking error within a range). By using multiple factors and rearranging portfolios, portfolio managers try to achieve this goal.

Factor analysis, or more broadly defined, quantitative analysis, has a long history, and sophisticated software is often used for its purpose. Many so-called quant analysts and portfolio managers spend their entire career bogged down in factor analysis.

"Those that conquer factors shall conquer the market" may not be too farfetched a statement, but the depth and width of the subject matter are well beyond the scope of this book. Accordingly, we will limit our discussion to a few crucial topics deemed important in understanding the Japanese equity market.

Since factors are the characteristics of individual stocks, any characteristic can be considered a factor (e.g., debt-to-equity ratios, the correlation between profit and foreign tourism, price sensitivity to the moon cycle). Employing all conceivable factors is impractical, however, and probably even meaningless, because many factors overlap and are dependent on one another. In general, therefore, the method taken is to conduct a factor analysis using more traditional factors and apply the obtained results to portfolio rearrangement.

In addition to factors such as the P/E and P/B described in the "Valuation and Technical Indicators" section in Chapter 4, traditional factors include the dividend yield, Beta (price sensitivity relative to index), profit momentum, price momentum, volatility, change in profit forecast, ROE, ROA, seasonality, and market capitalization. What factors are used in practice is left to the discretion of each portfolio manager and quant analyst.

These factors are also often categorized as value factors, quality factors, momentum factors, and technical factors, also used in selection of stocks or analysis of the market. The value factors are literally the factors used to judge how relatively "cheap" or "expensive" a stock is, the quality factors are used to isolate blue-chip names, the momentum factors allow us to judge if a stock possesses certain directional tendencies, and the technical factors are used to understand the technical aspects of a stock.

A typical factor analysis begins with isolating particular factors and examining how they performed over a certain period of time. Relatively uncomplicated, the process of isolation is done by first separating index constituent member stocks by their characteristics or factors, and then choosing, say, the top 10% or bottom 10% of those ranked by the particular factor.

Let us assume that the index is the Nikkei 225 Index (in reality, not many institutional investors use the Nikkei 225 as the benchmark). If we wish to look at the performance of the P/B as a factor, the process is to rank the index constituent stocks by their price-to-book ratio to select the top 20 names or so, and then to look at their collective performance by taking either the simple average or the weighted average.

In this process, if the names selected are too few, peculiarity rather than the common factor of the single stock will stand out and the factor return may become distorted. If too many names are selected, on the other hand, the factor performance itself becomes unclear. Generally, selecting the top 10% or so may be ideal, but there is no golden rule regarding this percentage.

Also, in conducting traditional factor analysis, the sector-neutral approach is often taken. This is because stock performance is often dependent on the sectors to which stocks belong (i.e., the sector itself functions as a factor). The sector-neutral approach is designed to eliminate sector influence by ranking stocks by factors from each sector, and thus to provide "purer" factor analysis and performance.

A word of caution here is that the sector-neutral approach also suffers from certain biases, as sector definitions vary from index to index. For example, the TOPIX 33 sectors are well-known and indexed, with some even equipped with their own futures. These sectors differ not only from larger sectors of the TOPIX but also from the MSCI Japan sectors.

Factor performance, needless to say, is affected by which index sector is being neutralized or whether any sector-neutral approach is taken at all. What we will see here are the results of the sector-neutral approach, using the MSCI Japan sector categorization. Using other index sector categorization may naturally lead to different results.

When investing in Japanese equities long-term, then, which factors should be favored? If we limit our argument to the period between January 2006 and January 2014, the best factor was the value factor.

More precisely, the P/B (investing in low P/B stocks on a monthly basis) produced the highest cumulative return, followed by the dividend yield (investing in high dividend yield stocks on a monthly basis). These results, actually, are true not just for Japanese equities but for US stocks and European stocks as well.

A low P/B means that the stock is sold to the extent that the price is cheap relative to its book value. A high dividend yield also means that the stock is sold such that its dividend is high compared to the stock price. In other words, the strength of the value factor simply suggests that the basic "buy-low-and-sell-high" investment strategy works well. It is no surprise that the strategy is viable in Japan, the US, and Europe.

What might be interesting is that the P/E, also a value factor, does not generate equally high returns. As we saw in the "Valuation and Technical Indicators" section in Chapter 4, for the "E" in P/E, usually forecast earnings are used. The poor P/E factor performance may indicate that investors are skeptical of consensus earnings forecasts particularly in time of market turmoil.

Next to the P/B and dividend yield, the factor that proved most effective was seasonality. In the "Seasonality" section in Chapter 1, the seasonality of the entire Japanese equity market was discussed. Just as the whole market possesses certain seasonality, so do individual equities. Since this is yet another major theme, we will look into it in detail later. Incidentally, the "seasonality" factor discussed here is identified by the average performance of individual stocks in a given month or season over the past several years.

The next effective factor after seasonality was the "change in profit forecast."

This factor is based on the strategy where investments are made in those stocks whose ratio of the past one-month's upward revisions by analysts over their downward revisions is high. Since analysts' views affecting stock performance are often observed phenomena, this should not come as a surprise, either.

Among the less effective factors are quality factors such as the ROE and ROA. The ROE stands for return on equity and is a ratio of net profit over total equity of the corporation. The ROA, likewise, stands for return on assets and is a ratio of net profit over total assets of the corporation.

Both of these factors measure how much profit is being made by the company relative to invested capital, and that is the reason why these are called "quality" factors. Put another way, the companies that make large profits relative to invested capital are deemed "quality" companies, and the quality factor measures the stock price performance of these companies.

Let us consider, then, why these factors are inferior in their historical performance. Once again, the principle of "buy-low-and-sell-high" reveals its rather dominant profile here. Note that the net profits used in the ROE or ROA are past numbers (the JPX400 Index, in selecting its constituent members, for example, uses the past 3-year average ROE). Naturally, corporations that made record profits in the past will likely have difficulty replicating their performance.

Equity investment, in essence, is an investment in corporate and profit growth, and hence investing in companies expected to have low growth or low profit improvement does not make much sense. Since companies with high ROE or ROA are largely those that have already achieved high returns and are deemed unlikely to report higher returns in the future, the ROE and ROA historical factor returns are almost perennially poor.

The changes in the ROE and ROA are also commonly used as factors, on the other hand, and perhaps unsurprisingly, they tend to perform better than either the original ROE or the original ROA, as they literally show how much improvement the corporations have made recently.

So far, we have looked at which factors worked well in the Japanese equity market in the long-term. Factor short-term performance naturally differs, as short-term performance depends much more on the state of the market of a period, whether bull, bear, or neutral.

A simplified picture is that in a bull market (particularly at an early stage), the factors that perform well are the beta and P/B, and in a later stage, the momentum factors such as the improvement in earnings forecasts and price momentum do well. In a bear market, as the words "flight to quality" suggest, quality factors such as the ROE and ROA, or factors such as the market capitalization and dividend yield tend to perform well. And when the market is about to turn either up or down, the reversion works well as a factor.

Momentum factors embody the expectation of past strength or weakness to continue into the future, and hence, their effectiveness in the market recovery phase is easily understandable. Reversion factors, in contrast, capture the change in dominant factors, and thus are most effective when the market turns from good to bad or vice versa. Regarding season-ality in factor returns, since the market as a whole possesses seasonality, so should factor returns.

Based strictly on past data, Table 5.1 summarizes the best- and worst-performing factors on a monthly basis.

In the following pages, the factors in Table 5.1 not yet clearly explained in this book are introduced.

1M Price Momentum: This factor is derived from the collection of stocks that showed the best price performance over the past 1-month period. As described earlier, the mother index in calculating these factors is the MSCI Japan Index, each factor isolated by taking the difference in returns between the top 10% and bottom 10% of the stocks. In calculating 1M Price Momentum, the stocks in the top 10% in monthly returns (about 30 stocks) are hypothetically bought and stocks in the bottom 10% are shorted to measure the factor performance.

12M Price Momentum: This factor is derived from the collection of stocks that showed the best price performance over the past 12-month period. The stocks in the top 10% yearly returns are bought and those in the bottom 10% are shorted to isolate this factor.

TABLE 5.1 Best and worst factors by month

	Best	**Worst**
January	P/B	1M Price Momentum
February	PCF	12M Price Momentum
March	P/B	1M Price Momentum
April	P/B	Market Cap
May	Sector-relative P/E	PCF
June	12M ROE Change	Beta
July	Earnings Momentum	Sector-relative P/E
August	60D Volatility	Beta
September	60D Volatility	Beta
October	ROA	1M Price Momentum
November	EPS Growth	PCF
December	Beta	60D Volatility and ROE

Source: MSCI

PCF: PCF stands for the price-to-cash flow and is a ratio calculated by dividing the market capitalization by corporate cash flow (totality of cash earned via business operation). Since market capitalization is largely in line with the share price, the PCF is a value factor, as are the P/E and P/B. The PCF is obtained by going long on low PCF stocks and shorting high PCF stocks.

Market Cap: Market cap stands for market capitalization and is obtained by multiplying the number of outstanding shares by the share price. Here, long are large cap names and short are small cap names.

Beta: Beta is a stock's sensitivity to a given index. If beta is 1, the stock is 100% correlated with the index. If beta is above 1, the stock has outperformed the index on the upside and underperformed on the downside. If beta is below 1, the opposite is true. The beta is based on past data, and here, a 2-year beta is being used. The factor calculation is done by going long on high-beta stocks and shorting low-beta stocks.

Sector-relative P/E: This factor is the P/E within a given sector. Low P/E stocks are bought and high P/E stocks are sold in the calculation.

12M ROE Change: This factor indicates the rate of ROE improvement in the preceding 1-year period. High improvement names are long and low improvement names are short.

Earnings Momentum: Earnings improvement over the preceding 3-month period is measured to calculate earnings momentum. The high earnings momentum stocks are long, and low ones are short.

60D Volatility: A stock's past 60-day volatility is measured for this factor (i.e., the 60-day historical volatility). Low volatility stocks are long and high stocks are short.

EPS Growth: EPS growth is calculated from the EPS (earnings per share) consensus forecast change from the previous fiscal year to the present fiscal year. High-growth stocks are the long names and low-growth stocks are short.

To repeat, the factors considered here are calculated by taking the spread between the simple average price returns of the long and short stocks.

When we draw conclusions from past data, we need to examine if the conclusions are simply accidental or make some reasonable sense. For example, the high correlation between the OECD CLI and the Japanese equity market, often cited in this book, is convincing not only because it is a historical fact but also because the OECD CLI is based on the economic data of the member nations. This should also be true for the factor return seasonality.

In the "Seasonality" section in Chapter 1, we saw that the December average return of the Japanese equity market was particularly strong, and the January return was far inferior. These statistics tell us to buy high-beta stocks at the beginning of December. Since low volatility stocks are generally diagonal to high-beta stocks, there is no surprise in seeing "60D Volatility" as one of the "worst" factors for December in Table 5.1. Also notable is the appearance of the quality factor, ROE, as the other "worst" factor.

In turn, the value factors such as the P/B and PCF are quite strong in January, February, March, and April, as opposed to the momentum factors. Stocks that performed well in November and December have performed poorly in January, particularly in recent years. Selling stocks that performed well up to that point (in other words, selling momentum) and switching into "cheap" value stocks is an example of a "reversion."

Also, that January is the beginning of a new fiscal year for most overseas investors is likely contributing to the factor return statistics, as buying "cheap" stocks makes sense in this context. Once again, the principle of "buy-low-and-sell-high" seems to be at work here.

The factor returns after the month of January appear to be plausible also. May is usually the month where the weakness sets in for the stock market. As a consequence, investors begin to look for cheap stocks within a sector. June and July represent the months where the annual results are announced for March-fiscal-end companies (recall that most Japanese companies have a fiscal year-end in March), and shareholders' meetings are also held then. Table 5.1 shows that factors related to corporate returns and profits are strong in these months.

August and September are the opposite of December. Since the market as a whole generally displays a poor performance in those months, low volatility stocks are bought and high volatility stocks are sold. Similarly, in October, the ROA, a quality factor, is dominant, and since the month of October often represents a turning point of the market, momentum is the worst factor.

November is the month where half-year results are announced for most companies. Once again, accordingly, the EPS growth exhibits a strong presence. When investors are focused on earnings results, price (value) factors appear to be less important, and hence, the PCF shows up as the worst factor.

We need to note that the results shown in Table 5.1 are based on "win ratio" rankings over the seven-year period from 2008 to 2015, and only the best and worst factors are listed. Factors that ranked second are not shown, but depending on the period of measurement, they could easily come into the list, and they, too, tend to be grounded in common sense.

In understanding factors, the importance of market sentiment and seasonality cannot be overstated. Behind every factor rotation, there is a change of season and market sentiment. In some sense, what we witnessed in Table 5.1 can be categorized as seasonal and sentiment rotations, rather than "pure" factor rotations.

How often, then, does factor rotation take place if we ignore market sentiment and seasonality? In an attempt to answer this question, we consider a strategy where we short the best factor and long the worst factor of one period in the period that immediately follows it. The periods tested are 1-month, 2-months, 3-months, 4-months, 5-months, and 6-months. If factor rotations are occurring with some regularity, though the worst factor may not become the best factor in the next period, it should record a positive return.

The backtests were performed from the end of May 2005 to mid-2014, and in all the cases considered, the returns were superior to that of the MSCI Japan Index. Particularly strong, however, was the 3-month return, which seems to suggest that factor rotations, in general, take place every three months in the Japanese equity market.

Once again, however, the strategy is not foolproof. When the market conditions are abysmal, the strategy actually backfires and the returns fall below that of the benchmark index. The periods from mid-2007 to end-2008, and 2011, after the earthquake, represent the time where investors saw the patterns of bad factors going worse and worse factors going worst.

In other words, while factor rotations do seem to take place every three months under "normal" conditions, there is a clear danger in blindly following this pattern. In order to optimize the return, therefore, we must take into account the market sentiment and seasonality, as before.

Sector Rotation

In the previous section, we saw that in the Japanese equity market, factor rotations generally take place every three months, and they also possess certain seasonality. In the analysis, a sector-neutral approach was taken, but sectors themselves display frequent rotations and possess certain seasonality as well.

Obviously, sector performance reflects the characteristics of the member stocks that the sector is composed of, and since the characteristics are defined by factors, there is a strong correlation between sector performance and factor performance. For example, the brokerage sector is represented by large brokerage firms, whose stocks are generally high-beta and high-volatility.

Regarding the frequency of sector rotation, there appear to be no definite patterns since the rotation largely depends on the market sentiment and themes of the time. When the economy is in a recovery phase, cyclical sectors may outperform for several months, and when the economy is on the downturn, defensive sectors are generally favored. Sector rotations also take place within the cyclical and defensive sectors themselves, again depending on the market sentiment, themes, seasonality, and valuations.

As discussed, sectors can largely be divided into cyclical and defensive. The cyclical sector is also called the economic-sensitive sector, and banks, auto manufacturers, machinery companies, electric appliance makers, steel and construction companies, real estate dealers, and brokerage firms, among others, are included in this category. As a rule, these sectors display higher price volatility.

The defensive sector, on the other hand, is less sensitive to the state of the economy. Sectors such as pharmaceutical, food, telecom, and land transportation typically belong in this category. As a rule, these sectors are low-volatility sectors.

We must note that these divisions and classifications are not etched in stone. On some occasions, ordinarily cyclical sectors can become defensive and defensive sectors can don the garment of high volatility. We recently witnessed this phenomenon in 2015.

The first quarter of the year 2015 was affected by asset allocation changes by the GPIF, as we saw earlier, but what dominated the market in the second quarter was a massive influx of tourist traffic from China. Media reports of Chinese tourists' buying up Japanese goods, ranging from electric appliances, cosmetics, and medicines to foods and clothing items, catapulted retail stocks, food stocks, and pharmaceutical stocks to their highs, lifting their valuations to bubble proportions from May to July. With the crash of the Chinese equity market in August, however, the bubble came to an abrupt end. The stocks and sectors usually considered defensive were aggressively sold off and thus suffered a dramatic surge in volatility in the second half of 2015.

Table 5.2 is the top 5 ranking of sector average monthly returns relative to the TOPIX, going back to 2004. Here, the sector returns are those of the TOPIX 33 sector indices.

The ranking is based on the average returns and thus is potentially influenced by any "abnormal" incidents or numbers. In addition, since sector indices are weighted by market capitalization, their performance is heavily affected by large-cap stocks within the indices.

Even with these caveats, many of the top 5 sectors appear to be there for good reason. It is also interesting to note that the ranking does not seem to be based on the earnings results alone but is often based on what may be "topical" for a given month.

Take the month of January, for example. It is the beginning of the year, and corporations and investors alike may be taking on new projects or strategies. Based on this reasoning, we may find it unsurprising to see the construction sector in the top spot for January, followed by the wholesale, marine transportation, mining, and air transportation sectors. Likewise, we may find it unsurprising to see the oil/coal sector at the helm for the month of February, the coldest month of the year in Japan.

March is not only the month of fiscal year-end for most Japanese companies but also the graduation month for most Japanese schools. It is a month where Japanese citizens prepare for the coming new school year, and corporations prepare for the new fiscal year. It may be easy to understand, therefore, why the consumer finance, warehouse/port, and retail sectors show their faces in the top 5 list.

Similarly, examples of social customs and weather affecting the sector performance may be seen in the month of August. There, August being the summer holiday month, the air transportation and land transportation

TABLE 5.2 Top 5 sectors in monthly returns

	1	2	3	4	5
January	Construction	Wholesale	Marine transport	Mining	Air transport
February	Oil/Coal	Marine Transport	Rubber Products	Iron/Steel	Insurance
March	Consumer Finance	Warehouse/Port	Retail	Metal Products	Other Products
April	Rubber Products	Real Estate	Consumer Finance	Oil/Coal	Fish/Agr/Frst
May	Marine Transport	Precision Instruments	Fish/Agr/Frst	Wholesale	Iron/Steel
June	Power/Gas	Land Transport	Construction	Warehouse/Port	Fish/Agr/Frst
July	Rubber Products	Precision Instruments	Pharmaceutical	Nonferrous Metals	Wholesale
August	Air Transport	Power/Gas	Pharmaceutical	Land Transport	Service
September	Rubber Products	Precision Instruments	Iron/Steel	Real Estate	Machinery
October	Real Estate	Construction	Consumer Finance	Automobile	Securities
November	Pulp/Paper	Securities	Textile	Power/Gas	Glass/Ceramic
December	Iron/Steel	Securities	Oil/Coal	Pulp/Paper	Warehouse/Port

Source: TSE

sectors are among the top performers. Additionally, increased usage of air conditioners may explain the presence of the power/gas sector in the list.

The weakness of the equity market as a whole in August may also explain the presence of low-beta sectors, such as power/gas and pharmaceutical, in the list. By the same token, the presence of the securities (brokerage) sector, a high-beta sector, may be explained by the strength of the overall equity market in November and December, as well.

Incidentally, what is "topical" for a given month appears to impact single stock performance also. If we examine the single stock performance data over the last twenty years, among the TSE1-listed stocks, the company that recorded the highest win ratio (highest ratio of positive returns) in the summer months of June to August is Kagome, a well-known fruit and vegetable juice maker.

Other high win ratio companies during those months are railway companies, beneficiaries of the summer holiday season. These companies may also be benefiting from the generally weak performance of the equity market as a whole, as was the case for the power/gas and pharmaceutical sectors.

Particularly interesting among "topical" performers may be those in the month of December. As reported earlier, December is the month where the Japanese equity market historically shows the best performance of any months, and the most effective factor is the beta.

From this fact, we may expect sectors that perform well in the month must be high-beta sectors, but as far as the win ratio is concerned, the top company is Ajinomoto, a food company. Because December is also a month where influenza often becomes "topical," the next in line is a pharmaceutical company, Eizai. Lixil, a company that specializes in home remodeling, stands together with Eizai with the same win ratio.

Stocks that follow these three are those of Yamato Transport, Nippon Meatpackers, Kikkoman, and Shionogi, all of which are generally low-beta stocks. From the standpoint of "topical" behavior, this may be an interesting phenomenon, as these companies are the beneficiaries of Japan's year-end gift-giving custom, home refurbishing, not to mention the influenza season.

Share Buybacks

In the "Factor Analysis" section above, we looked at the change in ROE as one of the factors. In the past several years, the low ROE among Japanese corporations relative to their peers in the US or Europe has become an issue for investors, and Abenomics certainly has not overlooked this factor. The introduction of the JPX400, whose selection criteria include ROE, exemplifies the government's effort to encourage Japanese corporations to improve their ROE.

To improve ROE, companies need either to increase the numerator R (net profit) or to decrease the denominator E (equities), or do both. It is clear, however, that cutting down on the number of equities is far easier than increasing profit in most cases, and this is where the share buybacks come in.

Since the end of 2012, when the second Abe administration effectively began, in 2014, 2015, and 2016, Japanese corporations bought back their own shares at record levels, but share buybacks were no strangers to them. Indeed, in 2006 and 2007, under PM Koizumi, Japanese corporations also engaged in aggressive share buyback programs.

In the investor statistics collected by the TSE, "corporate" refers to Japanese corporations, but most of the buying of Japanese equities conducted by them is actually share buybacks. Observing the Japanese equity market, we often witness a sudden elevation in the equity price as a share buyback is announced. This fact alone suggests that the share buyback is not an ignorable factor. In what follows, a few characteristics of share buybacks in the Japanese equity market will be described.

First, while not limited to the Japanese equity market, share buybacks tend to occur in tandem with improvement in corporate profit. When profit improves and cash becomes more readily available, corporations have more options in using their funds. They may decide to increase capital expenditure or increase the stock dividend for shareholders. Share buybacks are also one of the options.

A characteristic that can be pointed out is the recent trend of relatively high ROE companies conducting share buybacks. We may be witnessing these companies' efforts to maintain their already high ROE levels.

The recent data also suggests that share buybacks are not necessarily alternatives to a dividend increase. In 2012, 47% of the TSE1-listed companies that conducted share buybacks also increased their dividends. In 2013, the ratio rose to 59%; in 2014, 62%; and in 2015, 53%. What we see is that the share prices of these companies benefited not only from their

FIGURE 5.1 Number of corporations conducting share buybacks per month

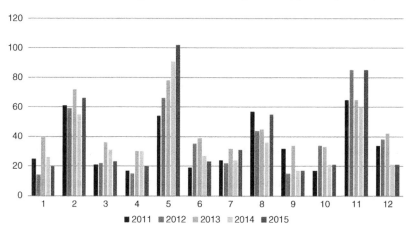

Source: TSE

earnings power but also from the mechanism of the share buyback and dividend increase.

The second characteristic of the share buyback in Japan is perhaps its seasonality. By looking at the data over the last ten years, share buybacks by the listed companies tend to rise in February, May, August, and November. Figure 5.1 shows the monthly number of TSE1-listed companies that conducted share buybacks from 2011 to 2015.

It is not difficult to imagine that the pattern of increase in share buybacks every three months is related to quarterly corporate earnings results. After taking into account their quarterly earnings results, companies are likely resorting to share buybacks.

If investors respond positively to the share buyback as a factor (more strictly, the announcement of the share buyback as a factor here), then if we know which company is going to announce share buybacks ahead of time, we can make an easy profit. In reality, however, unless we are insiders, this is a formidable task.

Let us see if we can isolate potential share buyback candidates by setting up what seems to be reasonable criteria. For example, one of the criteria we can use might be the concept of cash-rich companies.

Defining "cash-rich" by cash-held/market capitalization, if we look at the companies that conducted share buybacks in the year from January 2015 to January 2016, more than a half of those companies had less than 25% cash-held/market capitalization. In other words, companies do not necessarily have to be cash-rich to conduct share buybacks.

Also, as discussed earlier, companies with low ROE are not exactly the companies that conduct share buybacks. During the same January 2015 to January 2016 period, about half of the companies that bought back their own shares boasted above 7.75% 3-year average ROE.

What about companies with debt? Companies with a large amount of debt would rather pay out the debt than buy back their own shares, it would seem, but once again, this is not so. If we look at the cash ratio (cash or equivalent/payable debt), about half of those that conducted share buybacks during the above period had a cash ratio of less than 80%. We may note, however, that this statistic might have been skewed by the recent low-interest-rate environment.

We have also seen earlier that improved corporate profitability induces share buybacks. This is a macroscopic argument, however. Microscopically, improved profits do not necessarily induce corporations to buy back their own shares. Again, during the aforementioned one-year period, half of those that conducted share buybacks had an EPS growth rate below 6.3%, which was not a high number for that specific period.

One clear pattern that emerges is that the companies that conducted share buybacks in the past will tend to do so in the future. Share buyback, in a way, is a part of management philosophy. Thus, unless the whole management team gets replaced or the management decides to completely overhaul its style, a consistency in its philosophy is expected.

In what market environment, then, does the share buyback become the most effective factor? If we construct an index consisting of companies that conducted share buybacks in the past 1-year period and measure the index return against the TOPIX, in most cases we see outperformance taking place when the TOPIX was in the downturn.

An exception is the 3-year period following the introduction of Abenomics. During this period, led by government initiatives, raising ROE became something of a fad. Accordingly, the share buyback was recognized as an effective factor in the bull market.

Now that it appears the ROE fad may be coming to an end, the share buyback may no longer be an outperforming factor in a bull market. The likelihood is that it will resume its more or less defensive role.

Dividends

In the "Factor Analysis" section above, we saw that the dividend yield functioned as a defensive factor as well as a value factor. If the dividend is constant, the dividend yield is inversely proportional to the share price, and hence it serves as a value factor.

In this section, we will see the potential impact of dividend payments themselves, rather than dividend yield. Dividends, as a rule, are the way for a corporation to reward shareholders by offering a certain portion of its profit. This "portion" is called the dividend payout ratio, but not too many Japanese companies state a definite percentage in their annual reports.

Most companies that mention "payout ratio" in any form in their reports resort to stating that they will aim to maintain, say, above 20% or 30% payout ratio. Yet many other companies do not even state a specific percentage. They instead use expressions such as "We will strive for shareholder returns," or "We will endeavor to maintain a certain payout ratio."

In fact, many companies have constant dividend payment policies rather than constant payout ratio policies, since shareholders do not wish to see a decline in dividend payments, which are an important source of income.

Companies that do not readily lower dividends even in the face of adversity offer stable income to investors and thus are considered "defensive," but more popular are those that consistently raise dividends. (Dividend payment history for a given company can easily be obtained from data providers.)

There are quite a few companies in the US that have consistently raised dividends over the last twenty years, but in Japan, they are few and far between. Table 5.3 lists the annual simple average price returns of the stocks of companies that raised dividends for five years preceding period-ending years 2011–2016.

For comparison, the simple average returns of companies that consistently reported higher EPS, those that consistently increased total payouts (via either higher dividends, more share buybacks, or both), and TOPIX returns are also shown.

The returns of the companies that consistently raised dividends look quite impressive, though underperforming those that consistently increased total payouts in most years. Recall from the previous section

TABLE 5.3 Average annual returns of companies that consistently raised dividends, consistently reported higher EPS, and consistently improved total payouts

	FY2011	FY2012	FY2013	FY2014	FY2015	FY2016
TOPIX	–1.7%	21.2%	16.3%	28.3%	–12.7%	12.3%
Dividend	14.4%	33.0%	14.3%	38.3%	–4.8%	9.4%
EPS	7.3%	40.0%	23.8%	39.5%	–3.3%	8.1%
Total Payout	19.1%	50.3%	16.6%	64.6%	–6.6%	12.4%

Source: TSE

that those that conduct share buybacks will habitually tend to do so in the future.

Companies that consistently reported higher EPS are presumably equipped with excellent management teams and successful business models, both of which are likely conducive to even higher EPS in the coming years. In this book, limited emphasis has been placed on corporate earnings. This is not because earnings are considered to be "noise." This is because the share prices' going up and down with earnings or earnings forecasts is taken for granted and hence requires no emphasis.

The importance of Table 5.3 is that even though the backtest is based on the earnings in the preceding five years, the performance of those that reported higher EPS is generally superior at least in the following year to those that did not. In fact, the same can be said of fundamental measures outside of EPS.

For example, the share price performance of the companies with a high current profit-to-sales ratio (current profit/sales) has almost every year exceeded that of the companies with low current profit-to-sales ratio. This is true regardless of the direction of the market as a whole.

In the "Factor Analysis" section above, we saw that returns attributed to ROA and ROE (the numerators are the net profit in both) are generally inferior. There, however, we also saw that the change in ROA and ROE is often an effective factor. That observation is consistent with what we discussed here.

What may be more certain and easier to forecast than the EPS are the dividends, because they tend to have downside resiliency. In this sense, the companies that have consistently raised dividends are likely to do so even in a deteriorating economic environment and thus may prove to be a more reliable source of returns.

Stock Splits and Accessibility

Corporations often aim to enlarge the investor base by increasing accessibility to their shares (i.e., via increasing the existing number of shares by stock splits). The opposite is called reverse splits. In this context, "accessibility" refers to "ease of purchase," particularly for retail investors.

Take a case where the existing number of shares is 1,000 and the price is JPY1,000,000. If a 2-for-1 stock split is conducted, the number of shares will double to 2,000 but the price will be cut to JPY500,000, making the shares less expensive to buy. The increased number of shares also makes them more liquid and, thus, easier to trade.

These are the reasons why share prices tend to jump after stock split announcements. After announcements of reverse splits, in contrast, we generally witness share prices take a dive. Note that the word "announcement" is purposefully used here, as we may see contrary share price behavior upon the actual execution of a stock split or a reverse split.

Indeed, it is an often-observed phenomenon that a share price that rose immediately following a stock split announcement falls at execution. And not surprisingly, we also see that a share price that falls immediately following a stock split announcement often rises at execution.

Table 5.4 lists the statistics of the stocks that went through stock splits and reverse stock splits in 2015 and 2016. The top side is the TOPIX-relative performance after announcement of 2-for-1 and above splits, and the bottom side is the TOPIX-relative performance after announcement of 1-for-2 and below reverse splits.

As seen in the table, stock splits are generally positive for the equity price, but reverse splits are not. Since stock splits make shares easier to purchase and reverse splits make shares more difficult to purchase, the results in Table 5.4 offer no surprise. What we also see in the median figures in Table 5.4 is that most of the outperformance resulting from stock split announcements is achieved by the end of the first day.

In fact, upon closer examination of individual stock data, we can see that most of the outperformance is achieved within hours, if not minutes, of stock split announcements. Of course, the divergence between the

TABLE 5.4 Share price performance after stock splits (top) and reverse splits (bottom)

	1 Day	1 Week	2 Weeks	3 Weeks	4 Weeks
Average	5.4%	5.9%	6.4%	7.3%	7.5%
Median	5.3%	5.6%	5.2%	5.1%	4.9%
Average	0.2%	0.8%	0.7%	1.2%	1.6%
Median	0.0%	−0.3%	0.0%	0.3%	0.0%

Source: TSE

average and median figures tells us that some names continue to outperform even after several weeks, but such outperformance could be due to factors outside of stock split announcements.

Some other traits that became apparent by examining the data are the following: First, the effect of a stock split is felt more by small-cap stocks than large-cap stocks. Smaller stocks tend have lower liquidity to begin with, so they are likely to be more sensitive to increased liquidity due to stock splits. Additionally, since smaller stocks are scarcely covered by analysts, they may respond more sensitively to stock splits as a factor.

The second trait is that the larger the stock-split ratio, the larger the return after announcement. A stock split of 4-for-1 is naturally more impactful than 2-for-1, because the cut in share price is more dramatic. The third trait is that the returns after stock split or reverse split announcements are not subject to market sentiment as a whole. Whether the announcement is made during a bull market or bear market, notable divergence in TOPIX-relative performance was not observed.

In Table 5.4, we saw that, on average, the outperformance after a stock split announcement is mostly done within hours, if not sooner. If we know the general trend of companies that conduct a stock split before their announcement, therefore, we may be able to benefit from stock splits. One notable trend is that bull markets tend to bring out more stock splits. For corporations, the benefit of a stock split is to render their shares more accessible by bringing down the purchase price, and this is more likely to happen during bull markets.

Also, because the Japan Exchange Group, in order to keep shares more accessible to retail investors, is encouraging corporations to keep their share price between JPY50,000 and JPY500,000, the shares priced above JPY500,000 are more likely to be the target of a stock split. Additionally, since as with share buybacks, companies that conducted stock splits in the past tend to do so in the future as well, digging up the history of stock splits of individual companies is probably helpful.

A stock split announcement's leading to higher share price is directly related to increased accessibility (or the expectation thereof), but accessibility increase, obviously, is not limited to stock splits.

Table 5.5, by following a similar train of thought, looks at whether the difference in free float leads to alpha generation. In the "Impact of Index Funds" section in Chapter 3, we have seen that the MSCI conducts the annual free float (FIF) review at the end of May, every year. The "free float" discussed here actually refers to the free float ratio, which is subject to various corporate actions and thus requires occasional adjustments. The adjustments are needed since the indices are composed of just free float stocks and not non-free float stocks.

By the very definition of "free float," we should expect stocks with high free float ratios to have higher accessibility. We have already seen that money from passive funds go in and out of stocks at each index rebalance, and suckerfish investors attempt to take advantage of these phenomena.

Here, since we are not interested in the effect of index rebalance per se, but rather the effect generated by the difference in free float ratios,

TABLE 5.5 Share price performance according to free float factors

	FIF < 0.6	0.6 < FIF < 0.8	0.8 < FIF < 0.9	0.9 < FIF
Average	16.30%	10.80%	19.10%	23.50%
Median	9.70%	9.20%	16.30%	20.40%
Win Ratio	75.40%	66.70%	81.60%	83.90%
Avg Market Cap	1.51E+12	9.95E+11	1.49E+12	1.40E+12
FIF Adjusted Avg Market Cap	5.77E+11	6.80E+11	1.28E+12	1.30E+12
6M Average Volume	3.79E+09	3.78E+09	5.90E+09	7.98E+09

Source: MSCI

the returns listed in Table 5.5 are from June 2, 2016, to February 28, 2017 (during this time, the MSCI Japan Index rose 16.5%).

The sample size for FIF < 0.6 is 57, for 0.6 < FIF < 0.8 is 79, for 0.8 < FIF < 0.9 is 98, and for 0.9 < FIF is 87. Since the FIFs are different, the larger the FIF, the larger the index market capitalization, but among the samples tested, there was no significant bias in their market capitalizations. The divergence in the performance among the different FIF groups, therefore, is likely due to the difference in their trading volumes, and the general trend appears to be that the larger trading volumes result in better performance.

We note, however, that the better performance may be due to the measurement period's being largely a bull market. Had it been a bear market, we could have seen a worse performance for those with larger trading volumes.

As for sector bias, the sector-weighted average return was the worst for 0.9 < FIF, and the second worst was 0.8 < FIF < 0.9 (in other words, no particular sector was behind the superior performance of these two groups). From this, we may argue that sector bias also had limited influence in the group performance.

From these considerations, we may conclude that the free float difference, through the difference in accessibility, leads to the difference in trading volume, which in turn becomes the factor for alpha generation.

Natural Disasters

Natural disasters have many different faces, and their impact on the economy or stock market often does not reveal itself until several months or even years afterward. Obviously, the larger the scale of the disaster, the more impact it is likely to engender, but to quantify the correlation between the stock market and a natural disaster is nearly impossible, aside from the fact that the market rises and falls on news reports and speculations, and volatility spikes accordingly.

It is therefore doubtful that considering the impact of natural disasters will aid in making future investment decisions. When we think of the market as a mirror of the human psyche, however, examining how the market moved in the face of a major natural disaster should at least have some academic value.

As a case study, the Great East Japan Earthquake and Fukushima nuclear accident in 2011 will be discussed in this section. These incidents, together regarded as the worst crises of postwar Japan, may provide important historical lessons, as their scale was unprecedented and their impact was global in magnitude.

I was working on the trading floor at the time and remember clearly what took place before and after the initial onset of the earthquake. Also, as the gravity of the Fukushima nuclear accident became apparent, I was asked by the management, which regarded my graduate degree in nuclear physics as something of value, to take charge in analyzing the situation from the perspective of the security of the employees as well as the direction of the stock market. What follows in this writing is based on this experience.

When a colossal earthquake, which has come to be called 3.11, struck northern Japan on March 11, 2011, it set off a series of unfortunate events. On that day, I was busily preparing my weekly report at my desk, located on the 31st floor of an office building that looked down on Tokyo Station and toward Tokyo Bay beyond. The magnitude of the earthquake was originally reported to be 7.9 on the Richter scale. It was then revised up to 8.4 and 8.8. The 8.8 Richter in Japan, already an unprecedented level, was ultimately scaled upward to 9.0.

The news report of trouble at the Fukushima Daiichi Nuclear Power Plant was out on the first day. "The earthquake caused the stoppage of the power generator used for the cooling system" was what was reported.

Although no leakage of radioactivity outside the power plant had been detected, in accordance with the Act on Special Measures Concerning Nuclear Emergency Preparedness, the government nevertheless instructed the residents within the 3km radius of the power plant to evacuate the area.

The entirety of the catastrophe did not become clearer until the following day, Saturday, March 12, as TV viewers were constantly bombarded by the scenes of the horrific tsunami wiping out the coastal regions of the whole Tohoku area. Adding to the already devastating situation was the news of worsening conditions at the Fukushima Power Plant. Repair of the cooling system had run into some difficulties, according to the report, and the evacuation radius was expanded to 10 km.

That afternoon, the Nuclear and Industrial Safety Agency (NISA) mentioned for the first time the possibility of a meltdown in Reactor 1 of the

Fukushima Daiichi Power Plant. The nuclear power plants were safe, so we had been told, but the earthquake damage had ominously reached to the fuel rods in the core of the plant.

All the reactors at the Fukushima Daiichi Nuclear Power Plant were inactivated, but without the cooling system, the water in the reactor could evaporate, exposing the fuel rods. This is what leads to meltdown. Because the news report suggested that the possibility of meltdown existed not only in Reactor 1 but also in Reactor 3, the viewers were beginning to turn their suspicious eyes toward the government.

Does TEPCO, the operator and manager of the Fukushima Daiichi Nuclear Power Plant, have the knowhow to contain the situation? Is the government, in fear of causing panic, hiding the truth? At this point, the media was beginning to compare the accident to Three Mile Island and Chernobyl.

According to the NISA, the Fukushima Daiichi Nuclear Power Plant accident ranked at level 4 on the International Nuclear and Radiological Event Scale (INES). The Three Mile Island accident in 1979 was level 5, and Chernobyl in 1986 ranked as level 7, the worst in history. If the judgment of the NISA had been correct, the ongoing accident in Fukushima would have been far from the worst, but what the future would hold was anyone's guess.

On Monday, March 14, the Tokyo Stock Exchange opened for business as usual, resuming its normal and regular operations. Due to the lack of power generation stemming from the stoppage of the nuclear power plant, TEPCO had earlier begun to limit power supply to the public, which, compounded by the already quake-disrupted railway traffic, kept many workers from commuting to their offices and factories.

The Fukushima nuclear accident was already reported widely in the overseas media, but the content of the reports, perhaps to garner the greatest number of viewers, largely incited fear and paranoia. Indeed many "specialists" argued on television broadcasts that Fukushima was the second Chernobyl.

By this time, I was in possession of a 10-page report titled "Analysis of Fukushima Nuclear Power Plant Accident," put out by a US private consulting firm on nuclear matters. As the main argument, the report stated, "The radioactive materials exhausted out of the Fukushima Power Plant will become non-toxic within a matter of hours, as their half-life is short." My task, as a company man, was to judge the accuracy and plausibility of this report.

The report was concise and yet convincing; the writer was an architect of nuclear reactors and was part of the team that dealt with risk management and aftercare of the Three Mile Island accident. The worst conceivable outcome would be a meltdown, but even in such an occurrence, the damage to the environment should be limited, according to the report. The conclusion was that the so-called China Syndrome could not take place. (China Syndrome refers to a meltdown so severe that it goes through the core of the earth to the other side. Viewed from the US, the other side is China, hence the nomenclature.)

Had all of us known about and believed in the expert view offered in that report, the equity market would probably have stopped falling. On the other hand, the media—overseas and domestic alike—continued to bombard the public with sensational and often misguided opinions. "We are in a serious crisis," they said. "We are in dire conditions," we were told. No one had yet explained, however, how serious the crisis was or how dire the conditions were.

Should Tokyo residents leave the city? In the midst of conflicting information, the French government issued an evacuation warning to French nationals residing in Japan. According to the French, the Fukushima nuclear disaster was already up to level 6. In contrast, what we heard from the Japanese government was a nebulous statement: "It is not yet at levels hazardous to the human body." Did "not yet" mean it could be hazardous the next day?

The Nikkei 225 fell 6.2% on that day close to close. The magnitude of the fall was the largest single-day fall since the financial crisis in 2008.

Anyone who lived in Japan at the time could testify that the information on the nuclear accident released for days by the government was largely useless. The media was pretty much useless as well; they recycled "critical situation" and "serious problem" without ever elaborating on how "critical" and "serious" things were.

The lack of reliable information kept the public suspicious of the government's coverup of a reality far more serious than anyone might have imagined. We all found out later that, in truth, the government itself did not know what was going on. The suspicion nevertheless engendered paranoia, thrusting the Japanese fear index, VNKY, to its peak. As a result, the Nikkei 225 ended up plummeting a remarkable 10.6% close to close on March 15.

As countless aftershocks assaulted the city, with the exodus of evacuees under scarce guidance and without electricity, Tokyo turned into

FIGURE 5.2 Nikkei 225 movement before, on, and after 3.11

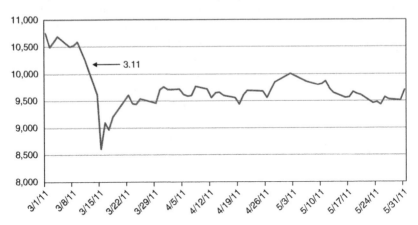

Source: FRED

a virtual ghost town. To this day, it is a mystery why the Tokyo Stock Exchange went about business as usual.

Figure 5.2 shows the movement of the Nikkei 225 around the time of the earthquake and nuclear accident. On March 11, since the earthquake did not strike until fifteen minutes before the market close, the Nikkei 225 drop was limited to 1.7%, but as the gravity of the nuclear accident became evident over the weekend, the drop extended to 6.2% on March 14, and as stated earlier, to a level even worse on March 15.

What might be interesting is the move on March 16. The Nikkei 225 rebounded 5.7% close to close on that day, which seemed odd because the end to the nuclear accident was nowhere in sight. What was behind this move might have been overseas quant funds and program traders that automatically bought stocks that were technically oversold or cheap in terms of valuation. To wit, when we view the record of investor activity at the time, foreigners were the chief and practically the only buyers of Japanese equities.

The movement of the Nikkei 225 afterward, however, probably could not be explained by technical measures alone. The index fell back on March 17, only to rise the following two days in a row. Then, until the beginning of May, the Nikkei 225 fluctuated within a narrow range between 9,500 and 9,750.

Since the extent of damage to the Japanese economy due to the earthquake and nuclear accident was not at all clear at that point, it might not be difficult to understand why the index did not rise. Why the index did not fall amid the rumors of meltdown is perhaps more puzzling.

The repetition of "the situation is not yet hazardous to human health" by the government was certainly not what investors based their judgment on. Even more certainly, investors were not listening to the inconsistent media sensationalism.

If anything worked, it might have been the will of the government to ensure that the general public did not panic, and thus, for example, the Tokyo Stock Exchange operated unimpeded. Indeed, foreigners were praising the Japanese people for their calm and restrained behavior in the face of the monstrous catastrophe. The very fact that the Japanese populace—those who should have feared the most—were so well-behaved was nothing short of amazing, which might have offered particular solace to foreign investors.

What played a larger role, however, might have been the true expert opinions, as expressed in the report I referred to earlier. Indeed, the view that Fukushima could not be a repeat of Chernobyl and that the ongoing situation would eventually be contained was not limited to the report in my possession.

In a press conference sponsored by the Japan Nuclear Technology Institute at the Foreign Press Club, a man in charge of designing the first nuclear reactor in Japan pounded the table and stressed, "At Three Mile Island, they succeeded in achieving steady state in a week. Fukushima might take a little longer but will nevertheless succeed." His view was that even the fuel rods in the storage pool should not matter, as the nuclear decay heat chilled down rapidly.

A professor of reactor engineering at the Tokyo Institute of Technology stated, "I let my kid play in the playground in the neighborhood. Most of my colleagues live in Tokyo and Kanagawa, but none of them is talking about fleeing the area."

These experienced and knowledgeable views render the rebound of the Nikkei 225 from March 15 and the stability of it since then not all that unnatural or unreasonable. Of course, with contradictory pieces of information flying back and forth, forecasting the index moves after 3.11 would have been practically impossible.

Looked at closely, however, sector moves appear quite reasonable from the viewpoint of the earthquake and nuclear accident. Table 5.6

TABLE 5.6 TOPIX 33 sector performance from March 10 to April 1, 2011

Sector	% change
Power/Gas	−27.5%
Real Estate	−14.4%
Insurance	−13.4%
Air Transportation	−12.7%
Consumer Finance	−12.5%
Banks	−12.3%
Fishery/Agriculture	−12.1%
Securities	−11.5%
Service	−9.3%
Marine Transportation	−8.8%
Retail	−7.9%
Automobile	−7.7%
Foods	−7.2%
Land Transportation	−7.0%
Pulp/Paper	−6.6%
Communications	−6.1%
Electrical Appliances	−5.4%
Precision Instruments	−5.2%
Other Products	−4.6%
Chemicals	−4.5%
Warehouse/Harbor	−4.5%
Textiles	−4.4%
Pharmaceuticals	−4.4%
Nonferrous Metals	−4.2%
Oil/Coal	−2.8%
Rubber Products	−2.2%
Iron/Steel	−2.0%
Glass Ceramics	−0.4%
Machinery	0.0%
Wholesale Trades	0.7%
Metal Products	4.3%
Construction	7.0%
Mining	13.5%

Source: TSE

ranks the TOPIX 33 sectors by the returns recorded from the close of March 10 to the close of April 1, in ascending order. During this period, the Nikkei 225 was down about 7%. The power/gas sector unsurprisingly ranks at the top (i.e., was the worst-performing sector), because the sector consists of power companies forced to halt the operation of their nuclear power plants after the Fukushima nuclear accident was initially reported, among which was TEPCO, whose role in the accident was under close scrutiny.

It is also not surprising to see the real estate sector ranked second, as the unending aftershocks and nuclear accident delivered a severe blow to the price of real estate in Tokyo and the surrounding areas. Insurance companies, expected to pay for the unprecedented damages, ranked in the third spot. In the more positive category, we see many sectors likely to benefit from energy needs alternative to nuclear power and recovery efforts from earthquake damages.

The Great East Japan Earthquake was indeed an ominous incident that saw too many deaths and too much suffering, but Table 5.6 at least suggests that, in the midst of the falling equity market and the peak of chaos, investors still behaved in a sensible manner.

CHAPTER 6

September 2017–December 2018

A s stated in the introductory chapter, much of the contents of this book is based on what I learned as an equity derivatives strategist specialized in the Japanese equity market. Needless to say, the market has continued to move since my retirement in August 2017, possibly providing us with an opportunity to examine the validity of many of the claims made and conclusions reached in the earlier chapters of this book. This chapter is dedicated to that purpose.

Backdrop

The Japanese equity market from September 2017 to December 2018 may be characterized by the effect of politics, internal and external, and interest rates, perhaps more so than most other years. Internally, PM Abe was saddled with the accusations of political favoritism said to be bestowed upon his "personal friends" (these incidents are known as the Moritomo and Kakei Gakuen scandals in Japan). Because of these accusations, in 2017 and 2018 his approval ratings dropped to the lowest level since he took office, according to multiple opinion surveys.

External politics played a major role because of North Korea, China, and Trump administration policies, though not, of course, in a mutually exclusive way.

As significant a threat to US security as North Korea was, the threat early in Donald Trump's presidency was more immediate to Japan than to the US due to the obvious geographical proximity of North Korea to Japan. Had the US and North Korea continued to escalate their threatening rhetoric, the Japanese equity market could have seen a different scenario. For the Abe administration, however, the threat was also something of a red herring, as public attention was diverted from his aforementioned potential political scandal.

The public generally viewed Abe to be a hard-nosed right-wing politician on good terms with President Trump, who spearheaded a demand for the denuclearization of the Korean Peninsula. It was not surprising, therefore, to see that each time North Korea conducted nuclear testing or launched a missile, Abe's approval rating jumped. Since PM Abe is the lynchpin of Abenomics, higher approval ratings of his administration have tended to foster a positive impact on Japanese equities.

Nevertheless, as was the case with the US equity market confounded by Richard Nixon and his Watergate scandal, Abe's approval ratings appeared to have had only a secondary impact on the Japanese equity market. What primarily did sway the market was economic reality and expectations, resulting from policy and political decisions made overseas.

As for China, Donald Trump's "America first" policy clearly had a negative impact on China's stock market, if not the whole economy. The tariffs repeatedly imposed on a variety of products moving out of China into the US pounded the nation's equity market, with the Shanghai Composite plummeting to its four-year low in August 2018. The collapse of the Chinese equity market, however, appeared to have only limited impact on the Japanese equity market for the first nine months of 2018.

In fact, although the threat and onslaught of a trade war between the US and China were believed to be a detriment to the global economy and equity markets around the world, in the twelve-month period from September 2017 to October 2018, the impact seemed largely negligible for most developed markets. By and large, this is particularly true for the US market.

In understanding the equity market of September 2017–December 2018, be it in the US or Japan, we cannot get past the Tax Cuts and Jobs Act that was signed by President Trump and that went into effect in December 2017. The tax cuts are the largest in US history, expected to total USD 1.5 trillion over a ten-year period. The act lowers the federal corporate tax rate from the previous 35% to 21% and also lowers the individual income tax (until year 2025) for most taxpayers.

The act is designed to create jobs for American workers by enticing overseas US corporations back to the US, corporations that avoided operations in the US due to higher corporate taxes. The act is also designed to encourage corporations with extra cash to boost capital expenditure and raise worker salaries, not to mention pay higher dividends to investors and possibly conduct more share buybacks.

The impact of the act was almost immediately felt. By January 2018, Apple announced that it would hire 20,000 more workers domestically and invest USD 30 billion in the US over the next five years. Comcast paid USD 1,000 bonus to more than a hundred thousand of its employees and simultaneously announced its plan to invest USD 50 billion in infrastructure over the next five years. Walmart raised its minimum hourly wage, from USD 10 to USD 11, as did Wells Fargo, from USD 13.5 to USD 15. Indeed, well over a hundred US corporations announced some sort of increase in minimum wage or investment.

All these actions looked wonderful at face value. There were potentially negative side effects, however, one of which leads us to another major player in the market, the US interest rates. Those of US long-dated treasuries in particular affected the global equity markets, including Japan's.

Interestingly, in forecasting the future growth of the US economy during the period, the Fed on the whole ignored the potential threat to the US economy posed by the trade war between US and China. The equity market largely shared the Fed's view of the strong US economy, as did the US bond market, evidenced by the long-dated yields' maintaining their upward trajectory for most of the period.

A strong economy does not always offer a rosy scenario, however. One of the worries in this case was that the US economy might become overheated, generating inflationary pressure and impetus for the Fed to hike interest rates more aggressively.

Indeed, the Fed continued to raise rates in 2017 and 2018. As the US economy prospered for most of the 2017–2018 period, the Fed made the decision to hike FFR, with the number of hikes totaling three in 2017 and four in 2018, pushing the effective FFR from 0.66% to 2.44%.

Another worry was that tax cuts would lead to a larger fiscal deficit for the US government, possibly leading to increased issuance of US treasuries. Concerns were that these possibilities would likely invite a selloff in bonds, catapulting long-dated interest rates to levels not seen in recent years. Higher rates generally put the brakes on the economy and act negatively on the stock market.

It was these negative side effects and materialization of the impact of the US-China trade war that eventually brought down the global equity markets in 2018.

In January 2018, the technically overheated Japanese equity market, along with the US equity market, began its nosedive, with the Nikkei 225 losing over 10% of its value in a matter of two weeks. The apparent culprit behind this precipitous fall was the US interest rates (to be examined in detail below).

The market regained its footing during the summer months of 2018 only to be slammed again by the US interest rates in October (the Nikkei 225 dropped 11% in fifteen days). The 11% fall formed a technical and temporary bottom of the market, giving investors a hope for the proverbial "Halloween effect" and strong December equity performance. This was not to be, however, as the problem for the market was compounded by a succession of significant and telltale events.

The first such event was the US midterm election held on November 6, US time. After a record turnout, the election created a Democrat-controlled House and Republican-controlled Senate for the first time since 1987. While the new balance of power obviously was going to make it more difficult for President Trump to push forward with his bold economic policies, the initial reaction to the election result was not a negative one, as seen in the performance of the S&P 500 the next day.

The equity market sentiment, however, quickly worsened by a microscopic factor—a downward profit forecast revision by Lumentum Holdings, a provider of optical components to telecommunications equipment makers such as Apple. Even before the downward revision, a slowdown of iPhone demand had been largely discounted in the market, but the severity of the slowdown was obviously not.

Here, what was later coined "Apple Shock" reared its ugly head as the materialization of the US-China trade war. As a result, so-called Apple-related stocks were sold off heavily in Japan in addition to the US, effectively ending what seemed to be immunity from the Chinese economic malaise for the first ten months of 2018.

The ill effect of the US-China war on the equity market did not end there. On December 1, Meng Wanzhou, CFO of Huawei, a Chinese telecommunications equipment giant, was arrested on Canadian soil for a charge that she helped her company to circumvent US sanctions on Iran. While the true reason for the arrest was still being disputed, the reaction of the market was swift and dramatic once the news of the arrest became public. Regardless of the substance behind the charges made against Ms. Wanzhou, the symbolism was that the US-China trade war was here to stay, with no quick fix in sight.

The decline of 770 points (3.5%) in the Nikkei 225 in the four days after news of the arrest can probably be attributed to concerns over the potential escalation of the US-China trade war, but the further decline that ultimately took the Nikkei well below 20,000 on Christmas day seemingly had two different causes.

The first likely cause was the data of US manufacturing PMI released by IHS Markit on December 14. While IHS Markit is a privately owned survey institution and its data sometimes diverges from the official ISM data, market followers often pay close attention to it as a precursor to the official number.

The December Markit US manufacturing PMI came in at 53.1, below the market expectation of 55.1 and a 2.2-point decline in the November 55.3 number. As with the ISMPMI, the fact that the number was above 50 still showed the expansion of the US economy, but the notable decline in the PMI suggested a potentially drastic slowdown in the US manufacturing sector. Here again, the US-China trade war might have begun to cast its long shadow on the US economy.

The second likely cause was the Fed. On December 20, the Fed raised the FFR target range by 0.25%, from the previous 2.00–2.25% to 2.25–2.50%. The move was largely expected, but, as discussed in "The Fed" section in Chapter 2, interest rate hikes in the face of a weakening economy can deliver a critical blow to the market.

In addition, what troubled the market was the expressed stance by the Fed Chair Jerome Powell, who announced that the Fed would likely continue to raise rates in 2019. The S&P 500 dropped 2.7% the next day, and with Japan a day ahead of the US and on holiday on December 24, the Nikkei 225 plummeted over 1,000 points (5.0%) on Christmas day.

Let us now put these pieces of background information together, along with what has been said about the Japanese equity market so far in this book, and look at the equity market from September 2017 on.

Japanese Equity Market

Figure 6.1 compares the Nikkei 225 with the S&P 500. By looking at the comparison, we are instantly struck by the similarity between the two. As the factors that drove the market identified above suggest, the similarity did not come from the S&P 500's mimicking the Nikkei 225 (or TOPIX), but the other way around.

There are, however, periods with notable differences. The first such period is from early September 2017 to early November 2017. While both the Nikkei 225 and S&P 500 had positive September and October performances, betraying the average seasonality patterns discussed earlier in the book, the Nikkei 225 performance was far superior to that of the S&P 500 (the Nikkei 225 was up 16.75% from August 31 to November 7, while the S&P 500 was up only 4.8% in the same period). Indeed, the Nikkei 225 at one point rose 16 days in a row for the first time in history, renewing its 26-year high.

FIGURE 6.1 Nikkei 225 and S&P 500 from September 2017 to December 2018

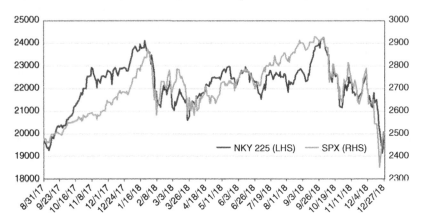

Source: FRED

A single dominant factor behind this impressive outperformance of the Nikkei 225 was the currency. As discussed in the "FX and the Japanese Equity Market" section in Chapter 2, a weaker Japanese currency generally entails a robust Japanese equity performance. The JPY weakened against the USD by 3.6% from August 31 to November 7. Thus, even in the USD terms, the outperformance of the Nikkei 225 over S&P 500 was some 13%. Unsurprisingly, the outperformance halted on November 7, when the USDJPY peaked and turned around.

Thus, the currency factor apparently remained valid in this instance. What drove the JPY weakness and the simultaneous outperformance of the Nikkei 225 remained the same as well.

A similar pattern was also observed in 2018. For example, the USDJPY began to fall from 113.2 on January 8 to 104.9 on March 26, and in the same period, the Nikkei 225 dropped over 3,000 points, losing almost 13% of its value. The USDJPY then gradually bounced back to 114.5 on October 4, during which time the Nikkei rose about 3,200 points or 15.5%. The subsequent collapse of the Nikkei was also accompanied by a notable decline in the USDJPY until January 3, 2019. Although the peaks and troughs of the USDJPY are not perfectly in tune with those of the Nikkei, the correlation between the two is unmistakable.

FIGURE 6.2 ISMPMI from January 2017 to December 2018

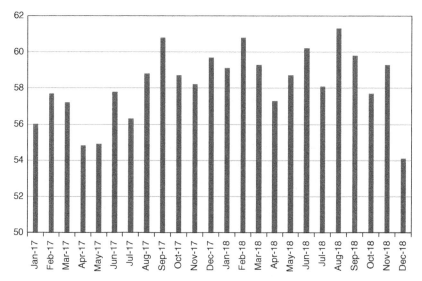

Source: ISM

Figure 6.2 shows the trend of the ISMPMI from January 2017 to December 2018. As stated earlier, an ISMPMI above 50 means that the economy is expansionary and below 50 recessionary. In this regard, we see that the US economy was in an expansionary state throughout 2017 and 2018. Recall, however, that what is more important for the equity market is the "change" in economic indicators rather than their absolute levels.

We note in Figure 6.2 a sudden jump in the ISMPMI from July to August 2017. Since the August number was released on September 1 (September 2 Japan time), it did not have an effect on the Japanese equity market until September 4 (September 2 and 3 fell on Saturday and Sunday).

In the "ISMPMI" section in Chapter 1, it was stated that a jump in the ISMPMI, on the average, does not generate a jump in the Japanese equity market. But this is "on the average." Since both the Nikkei 225 and S&P 500 had a very mediocre performance for the first eight months of the year, investors could have taken the jump in the ISMPMI as the first and decisive green sign to go ahead. Still, the Japanese equity market did not begin its outperformance, in coincidence with the JPY weakening, until September 11.

Why the delayed reaction? The chief drivers of the market this time were the foreign investors, as usual. Many of them were on summer break and thus possibly held investment strategy meetings in the first week of September. Nevertheless, it seems rather odd that they moved in unison at the same time. The Fed was not a factor at this time, either, since the FOMC meeting was not scheduled until September 19, and as it turned out, the Fed did not raise FFR until December 13.

What caused the delay, in my view, was North Korea.

With a succession of missile launches on August 26 and 29, followed by a nuclear test reportedly of a hydrogen bomb designed for ICBM on September 3, the tension between North Korea and the US reached an apex in the first week of September. Because of this, investors naturally remained "risk-off" at that time, holding their breath for a possible retaliatory action by the US. It was only after such a possibility seemed lessened that investors turned "risk-on" and began to invest aggressively in Japanese equities.

Another factor that likely contributed to the Nikkei 225 outperformance was the lower house election held on October 22. The lower house was officially disbanded on September 29, and the Nikkei 225 appears to have begun its spectacular climb from around that date. The election, in effect, was not only a referendum on PM Abe's ongoing economic and international policies but also a test to see how much Abe's popularity was damaged by political scandals.

As discussed in Chapter 2, "Policy Impact," the landslide victory by the LDP tended to push the equity market higher in recent history. The election result this time was that the LDP retained its majority seats in the lower house, giving the Abe administration an effective thumbs-up on its policies by the Japanese populace. The LDP victory had been forecast in the coverage of various media long before the actual voting, and the equity market responded accordingly.

By November 1 2017, the Nikkei 225 was technically overbought, and when the October ISMPMI dropped and the USDJPY reversed its course, the Japanese equity market recoiled. Almost simultaneously, the US equity market was picking up its pace, with the anticipation of the passage of the Tax Cuts and Jobs Act. Although the Nikkei 225 bounced back and renewed its post-1980s-bubble high on January 23, 2018, the S&P 500 outperformed the Nikkei 225 by 4.4% from November 7, 2017, to January 23, 2018. The so-called Goldilocks Market, where low interest rates and low rates of inflation coexist, appeared to last forever. But this was not to be. As described above, the Nikkei 225 began to plunge on January 24 and the S&P 500 on January 26, and within a matter of days, both markets lost more than 10% of their value.

While technical factors were unquestionably involved, the primary agent that brought down the market in this instance was none other than the US interest rates, and the incident was not an anomaly, as the phenomenon was repeated in October 2018. We will see how the US interest rates interacted with the equity market in the following section.

Going back to the ISMPMI, the December 2018 number (released on January 2, 2019) indeed mimicked that of the Markit PMI (the December 2018 ISMPMI fell 8.8% from the November number).

As seen in the "ISMPMI" section in Chapter 1, a large fall in this index generally spells trouble for the Japanese equity market. It was therefore not surprising to see the Nikkei falling 450 points on the first trading day of the year 2019. Technically, however, the Japanese equity market was "oversold" as of December 25, which might be one of the reasons why the Nikkei remained above 20,000 for the rest of January 2019.

Interest Rates and Equity Market

As we saw in "The Fed" section in Chapter 2 and elsewhere in the book, interest rates play an important role in the equity market. This is also obvious in various textbook equity valuation models, such as the dividend discount model, cashflow discount model, and the like, since what these models have in common is the risk-free rate in the denominator, which, in general, is the government bond yield (e.g., for US equities, US treasury yields).

In "The Fed" section in Chapter 2, the main focus was the short-dated interest rate or more precisely, the Federal Fund Rate (FFR). When we were looking at the negative interest rate policy (NIRP) by the BoJ, the focus there was also short-dated deposit rates, although we saw that short-dated interest rates and long-dated rates tend to move in the same direction.

A textbook interpretation of the relationship between interest rates and the equity market goes like this: The short-dated and long-dated interest rates tend to move in the same direction because they are driven by the same factors.

When the economy is slowing down or outright recessionary, interest rates tend to be lower because the policymakers cut interest rates to stimulate the economy. Also, since investors become "risk-off" in recessionary periods, they tend to prefer bonds over equities, which lowers long-dated yields. (Recall that bond prices and yields are inversely related.)

When the economy begins to rebound, often inflation expectations pick up as well, and since any inflation is a detriment to fixed income instruments, bonds tend to get sold off, which pushes up long-dated yields. Accordingly, interest rates, particularly long-dated ones, tend to go hand in hand with the equity market (i.e., they rise and fall at the same time).

Herein lies the difficulty of using interest rates as a leading indicator for the equity market. Figure 6.3 depicts this difficulty well.

We see that, in general, the equity market (the Nikkei 225 in the present case) and the US 10-year treasury yield move in the same direction. There are clearly exceptions, however. In fact, as stated earlier, a

FIGURE 6.3 Nikkei 225 and US 10-year treasury yield

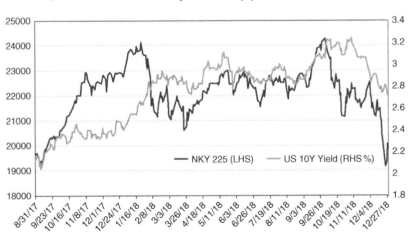

Source: FRED

common understanding is that the rise in the US 10-year treasury yield caused the big drop in the equity market in February and October of 2018.

By simply eyeballing the comparison between the Nikkei 225 and US 10-year treasury yield in Figure 6.3, we may say that what prompted the equity market plunge was not the absolute level of the treasury yield (the long-term interest rate). Rather, it was the speed at which the interest rate rose. As we saw in earlier chapters repeatedly, the market generally dislikes sudden changes.

Some argued after the February 2018 equity market plunge that the culprit behind the plunge was the yield spread. Yield spreads commonly refer to the spread between yields of bonds with differing maturities. The yield spread in this context, however, is calculated by the S&P 500 earnings yield subtracted from US long-term treasury yields (for all intents and purposes, the US 10-year treasury yield).

Since the earnings yield is the inverse of the P/E, the more expensive the equity market is, as measured by its overall P/E, the lower the earnings yield. When the treasury yield encroaches upon or even surpasses the earnings yield, therefore, equities become less attractive in relative terms.

As seen in Figure 6.4, the yield spread, for the first time in a long while, climbed above –2.0% in the early part of January as the long-term

FIGURE 6.4 US 10-year treasury-S&P 500 earnings yield spread

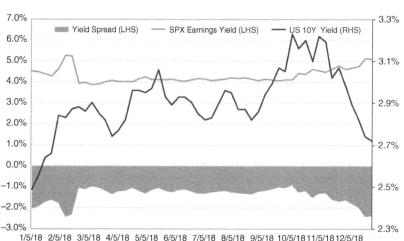

Source: FRED

yield began to rise. Calling the yield spread the culprit seems too much of a stretch, however, as the market collapse did not commence until about a month later. Indeed, both the S&P 500 and Nikkei 225 were already showing strong performance by early April, despite the yield spread remaining well above -2.0%.

Thus, it appears that the speed at which the treasury yield made the ascent was the more plausible culprit. Although the magnitude of the decline does not even come close, the phenomenon is akin to what took place prior to Black Monday on October 19, 1987. The US equity market was booming prior to Black Monday, and so was the US economy. Responding to the overheated economy and the threat of inflation, the long-term yields began their eerie ascent in September, followed by a sudden bolt in October, and the rest is history.

As implied earlier, however, the difficulty is that a sudden rise in the treasury yield does not necessarily lead to a collapse of the equity market. For example, the US 10-year yield rose from 2.41% on December 25, 2017, to 2.84% on January 29, 2018, but the Nikkei 225 rose 3.0% and the S&P 500 rose 6.5% in the same period.

In February 2018, much was made of the fact that the US 10-year yield rose above 3.0% for the first time since December 2013. Back then, the US 10-year yield went from 2.53% on October 21, 2013, to 3.01% on December 30 2013, but here again, the Nikkei 225 rose 10.9% and S&P 500 rose 5.9% in the same period.

These examples suggest that rising rates, though they may present a source of concern, perhaps by themselves should not be used in timing equity investments. Only when combined with valuations and technical and other factors do the rising rates present a threat to the equity market. Incidentally, the Nikkei 14-day RSI on January 23, 2018, right before the big drop, peaked at 81.2, and from October 2 to 4, right before the next market debacle, it remained well above 70, a technically overheated level (technical factors are discussed in the next section).

Once again, the Goldilocks Market came under serious scrutiny due to the two major equity market corrections we experienced in 2018. Should the long-term rates continue to rise going forward, we may conclude that the Goldilocks Market did not present a paradigm shift, as some market observers believed, but rather nothing but a temporary illusion.

Technical Indicators

The Japanese equity market, along with that of the US, may be characterized by high volatility in 2018, earmarked by the two giant drops that began in January and then in October. While what triggered the drops might have been the sharp rise in the US treasury yield, as discussed above, we also cannot ignore technical factors as significant contributors.

The claim made earlier in the text is that technical indicators have some success in determining market tops and bottoms, though they are by no means almighty. With this understanding, let us see how those technical indicators fared in pinpointing the correct "sell and buy" timings in 2018.

Figure 6.5 is the 60-day Bollinger Bands of the Nikkei 225, with two outside lines located at 2σ. At first glance, it appears that the Bollinger Bands served well in telling us when to sell and buy the Nikkei 225 in 2018.

To test our first impression, let us assume that we automatically sold the Nikkei 225 (via ETF or futures) as it reached the upper Bollinger Band

FIGURE 6.5   Nikkei 225 60-day Bollinger Bands

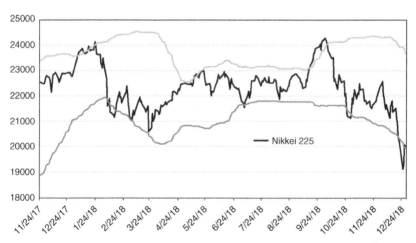

Source: FRED

and bought it back as soon as it reached the lower Bollinger Band. Here, we also assume that we do nothing to our position unless the Nikkei 225 hits either one of the Bollinger Bands; that is, if the Nikkei 225 hits either of the Bollinger Bands multiple times without touching the other, only the first such occurrence is counted as the signal.

The end result of this simple calculation is that investors would have realized 43% return as of October 25, as the Bollinger Bands signaled a "buy." Considering that the Nikkei 225 itself ended up on a loss, the Bollinger Bands approach proved to be an effective one for most of 2018. In a volatile market, where the index moves up and down at relatively regular intervals, this is largely expected.

The difficulty, as discussed in the text earlier, lies in the fact that we had no idea that the market would move up and down as it did in 2018. We could have had a market that moved more or less in one direction. In fact, the "buy" signal on October 25 ended up in a 5.9% loss at the year-end since the market collapsed and the Bollinger Bands failed to touch the upper band during the period.

The success of the Bollinger Bands leads us to suspect that other technical indicators must have recorded positive returns as well during the period. Using the Nikkei 14-day RSI, however, only generated 5% cumulative return up to October 15, and as of year-end, the unrealized loss of about 10%.

This result was obtained by using RSI > 70 as the "sell" signal and RSI < 30 as the "buy" signal. Needless to say, had we used different levels, the result could have been more positive. We could have also used, say, the 25-day RSI, rather than the 14-day RSI. All these considerations, however, are only after the fact, as was the case for the Bollinger Bands. They may only highlight the danger of blindly using technical indicators.

With regard to the Toraku ratio, recall from Table 4.2 that Toraku ratio > 130 and Toraku ratio < 60 generated positive results on the average (using the 25-day Toraku ratio). Since this measure would have generated only one inflection point in 2018, we need to relax the condition so that Toraku ratio > 120 is the "sell" signal and Toraku ratio < 80 is the "buy" signal.

The result thus obtained is the cumulative return of 58% up to December 17, although it failed to foresee the catastrophic drop of December 25. As impressive as the cumulative return might be, once again, this is only after the fact. Before 2018 started, we could not have known that Toraku ratio < 80 would give us an appropriate "buy" signal.

Another word of caution is that these results are only valid for close-to-close trades. In reality, much of the gain could have been lost by the open of the market or the signal could have occurred at the open or during the day so that close-to-close trades could have generated much inferior results compared to what we saw in these backtest results.

Incidentally, the Bollinger Bands, the 14-day RSI, the 25-day Toraku ratio, and the deviation from the 25-day moving average (the deviation was 10%) all signaled a "buy" on the Nikkei 225 on December 25. Judging from the market performance from that day on, the combined technical indicators functioned well in this instance.

Last but not least, let us see if the VIX Index could have "predicted" any of the large Nikkei downturns in 2018. Figure 6.6 shows that the notable spikes in the VIX Index are largely coincidental to the big drops in the Nikkei 225 or, more precisely, the big drops in the S&P 500.

We might assume that since the business hours of the Japanese equity market and US equity market are about fifteen hours apart, we can predict which way the Japanese equities are headed the day before. Indeed this works in many cases, but recall that most of the Nikkei moves take place during the Japanese night in the US market open hours so that investors generally cannot take advantage of the time differentials.

FIGURE 6.6 VIX Index from September 2017 to December 2018

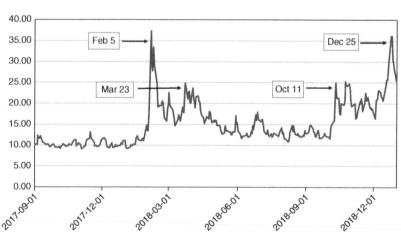

Source: FRED

In any event, once again, the conclusion that can be reached is that we cannot use the VIX Index or any other volatility measures to pinpoint big drops or spikes in the market.

Seasonality and the OECD CLI

The seasonality factor performance was something of a mixed bag in 2017 and 2018. Both the Nikkei 225 and TOPIX betrayed the summer weakness scenario in 2017, gaining over 14% from the end of April to the end of October, 2017. Subsequently, however, the Halloween effect was only marginally visible, with the Nikkei 225 gaining about 2% and TOPIX gaining less than 1% from October 31, 2017 to April 27, 2018.

Afterward, the summer weakness set in, with the Nikkei 225 losing approximately 2.5% and TOPIX losing about 7.5%. The discrepancy between the two key indices can be explained by the weights of constituent stocks in each index, where auto companies such as Toyota and other automakers, potential targets of future US tariffs, weigh heavily in the TOPIX.

Where seasonality betrayed us the most was toward the end of 2018. While the November Nikkei 225 performance turned in a positive return of about 2%, the December performance was an abysmal negative 10%. The Nikkei 225 recorded a negative return for the year as a result for the first time in seven years. In fact, we need to go back eighteen years before we can find a Nikkei marking a year-to-date low in the month of December.

As for the performance of the OECD CLI, perhaps the following explanation can be offered. Figure 6.1 illustrates how similar the paths taken by the Nikkei 225 and S&P 500 were for most of the September 2017–December 2018 period. The OECD CLI turned down for March 2017 (the number was released in May 2017) and as of December 2018 largely remained in its downward trajectory (see Figure 6.7). The Japanese equity market, in this regard, defied the pull of gravity by the OECD CLI and followed the US equity market leadership during most of the September 2017–December 2018 period.

As discussed in the "OECD CLI" and "More on OECD CLI" sections in Chapter 1, contrary to the Japanese equity market, the US equity market has historically shown poor correlation with the OECD CLI.

FIGURE 6.7 TOPIX and OECD CLI from January 2017 to December 2018

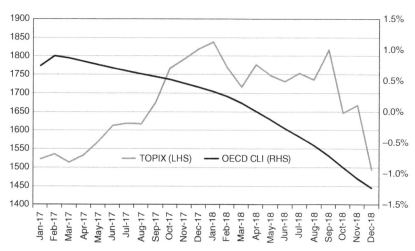

Sources: TSE, OECD

The way the Japanese equity market in the September 2017–
December 2018 period faithfully followed the US equity market, in spite
of the OECD CLI, may therefore be somewhat surprising. Recall the
argument from Table 1.3 that the OECD CLI usually does not get it
wrong unless some events or policy moves take place that defy economy
reality. If this argument still holds water, then the US equity market up
to the period ending in September 2018, at least, may be deemed a
"bubble" or something that does not reflect the economic reality.

The Buffett Indicator was one of the subjects alluded to earlier in the
text, and it may serve to partially explain the Japanese equity market performance over this period. According to this ratio, the US equity market
has been in a bubble-like state for quite some time up to September 2018
and may last even longer, possibly hoisted by the impact of the Fed's QE
and Donald Trump's Tax Cuts and Jobs Act.

On the other hand, robust US economic indicators, such as the
ISMPMI, seem to tell us that the US equity market performance is
perhaps justifiable. Since proverbially a bubble is not a bubble until it
bursts, however, the argument is probably moot.

What we know as a fact is that the OECD CLI largely failed to predict the direction of the Japanese equity market from May 2017 to at least September 2018. Whether the failure continues into the future is quite uncertain, as we witnessed the collapse of the equity market globally from October through December of 2018.

As of December 2018, the TOPIX is slightly below the level we saw before the OECD CLI turned down in May 2017. So, the OECD CLI may still "get it right" in the end (before it turns up). If it does, this example illustrates that equity investment sometimes takes patience before it turns profitable.

If the OECD CLI fails in the end, however (i.e., produces a negative return during its down period), the failure may entail two possibilities: 1. The Japanese equity market has lost its sensitivity to the global economy. 2. The OECD CLI no longer accurately reflects global economic conditions.

The first possibility is a matter of degree, because no equity market completely loses touch with the economy for an extended period. Only time will tell if the Japanese equity market will be more like the US equity market or retain its considerable sensitivity to global economic directions.

The second possibility may perhaps be more alarming, for it implies that the OECD CLI, one of the more reliable macroeconomic indicators, no longer functions. As stated in the "OECD CLI" section in Chapter 1, however, the OECD CLI is an end-product of dedicated scientific studies. As with any other scientific tools, the strength of the OECD CLI is that it is constantly monitored and adjusted, if need be, in an attempt to ensure that it accurately reflects economic reality. In this respect, the OECD CLI will likely get back on track, if it has, in fact, been derailed.

As depicted earlier, the poor equity market performance from the second leg down of October 2018 and onward is particularly intriguing, for the culprit no longer appears to be the long-term interest rates. The IMF downgraded its global economic outlook, specifically referring to the US-China trade war as the main cause of concern, and the world equity markets were rattled by its warning. Chief economic indicators globally began to show signs of ailment, not to mention the deterioration in the equity markets around the world, and we may still witness the prediction of the OECD CLI come true. Once again, time will be the judge.

Epilogue

In writing this book, my original intent was to create a book of history as well as case studies. I became aware midway, however, how in-depth and far-reaching the content would have to be to meet the original aim. My awareness aside, I did not have the luxury of writing forever, obviously, as the market changes and progresses every day. Investment reports are required to be timely as well as accurate, and books on investment should adhere to the same standards. In this sense, composing this book was a race against time.

While I was in the middle of writing this book, the Nikkei 225 rose 16 days in a row for the first time in history, renewing its 26-year high. Because the climb might have been triggered by the landside LDP victory in the autumn election, the market could have been titled "Abenomics Market III."

At the same time, the US equity market could not have been more robust, with the S&P 500 moving well beyond the Buffett Indicator of 1.0, possibly reaching a bubble-like stratosphere. The record low interest rates worldwide and ample cash generated by easy money policies apparently continued to display a positive (if the market is a bubble, negative) impact on the overall economy.

The Goldilocks Market seemed to conjure a paradigm shift, and I found it ironic that the OECD CLI, whose effectiveness is the mainstay of this book, did not work well in the market environment for more than a year after August 2017.

The Japanese equity market in the second half of 2017 may be characterized by the aforementioned election victory by the LDP; recovery in the US and Chinese economy; the Fed-BoJ policy rate differentials leading to the weaker-JPY trend and its potential benefit for Japanese corporations, which also enjoyed record retained earnings; and the phenomenal strength of the US equity market likely induced by the prospect of the largest tax cuts in history. The market surge we saw in November 2017 was likely the seasonality effect alluded to earlier in this text. When the direction of the economy is not clear-cut, often seasonality supersedes other factors.

I retired from the position of derivative strategist as of August 2017, but had I written a research report since, the tone undoubtedly would have been bullish after the landslide LDP election victory and would have continued to be so from seasonality and the passage of the US Tax Cuts and Jobs Act. This said, to be honest, I could not have guessed that the Nikkei 225 would reach a 26-year high.

Leaping forward to February 2018, the Goldilocks Market scenario came under question due to the rise in the US long-term interest rates. The equity market saw a major correction globally, only to be overshadowed by a far more serious correction in the last quarter of the year. As described in the text earlier, the culprit of the correction in the last quarter of 2018 was not only the long-term interest rates but also the apparent materialization of the US-China trade war.

In a sense, what may be called the "Trump factor" worked positively in 2017 but perhaps negatively in 2018. In fact, by the end of 2018, the TOPIX trade based on the OECD CLI would have generated a positive return for the 2017–2018 period.

This is the turn of events that prompted me to add the last chapter, titled "September 2017–December 2018," to the original text. This last chapter, I hope, gives a more up-to-date view on some of the topics encompassed in the rest of the text, and also confirms many of the claims made in the earlier chapters of the book.

As repeated many times throughout this book, the market rules and patterns are what we saw in the past and may not pertain to future markets. In principle, the market will continue to be the mirror of the economy as well as of the human mind, but with the increased role of AI in the market, these principles seem by no means absolute. Historically, the market has experienced paradigm shifts many times, and each time, investors had to adjust methodologies or create new ones. As long as investors are guided by greed and fear, this pattern will perhaps never change.

Needless to say, I do not believe that this book has covered all methods and formulae required to generate profits from the Japanese equity market. Many phenomena and subjects are not discussed, and probably some backtests described are not thorough enough.

As stated in the beginning, the market suffers from a large quantity of noise, and this book was written with the intent of eliminating noise as much as possible, but then again, what I consider to be noise may turn out in future to be the sound we should listen to. On this point, I stand in the court of judgment, willing to receive any criticism and praise that come my way.

Index

Page numbers for figures are given in *italics*, and for tables they are given in **bold**.

Printed and bound by CPI Group (UK) Ltd, Croydon, CR0 4YY

16/04/2025

14658500-0001